LawExpress
HUMAN RIGHTS

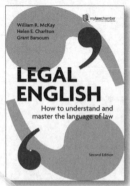

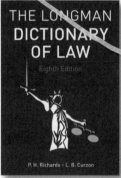

Law Express

HUMAN RIGHTS

2nd edition

Claire De Than
City University

Edwin Shorts
London Metropolitan University

PEARSON

Harlow, England • London • New York • Boston • San Francisco • Toronto • Sydney • Auckland • Singapore • Hong Kong
Tokyo • Seoul • Taipei • New Delhi • Cape Town • São Paulo • Mexico City • Madrid • Amsterdam • Munich • Paris • Milan

Pearson Education Limited
Edinburgh Gate
Harlow
Essex CM20 2JE
England

and Associated Companies throughout the world

Visit us on the World Wide Web at:
www.pearson.com/uk

First published 2010
Second edition published 2013

ISBN: 978-1-4082-7180-3

British Library Cataloguing-in-Publication Data
A catalogue record for this book is available from the British Library

Library of Congress Cataloging-in-Publication Data
A catalog record for this book is available from the Library of Congress

10 9 8 7 6 5 4 3 2 1
16 15 14 13 12

Typeset in 10/12pt HelveticaNeueLTPro by 71
Printed and bound by Ashford Colour Press Ltd, Gosport

Contents

Supporting resources

Visit the *Law Express* Series Companion Website at
www.pearsoned.co.uk/lawexpress to find valuable student learning material
including:

- A study plan test to help you assess how well you know the subject before you
  begin your revision
- Interactive quizzes to test your knowledge of the main points from each chapter
- Sample examination questions and guidelines for answering them
- Interactive flashcards to help you revise key terms, cases and statutes
- Printable versions of the topic maps and checklists from the book
- 'You be the marker' allows you to see exam questions and answers from the
  perspective of the examiner and includes notes on how an answer might be
  marked
- Podcasts provide point-by-point instruction on how to answer a typical exam
  question

Also: The Companion Website provides the following features:

- Search tool to help locate specific items of content
- E-mail results and profile tools to send results of quizzes to instructors
- Online help and support to assist with website usage and troubleshooting

For more information please contact your local Pearson Education sales
representative or visit **www.pearsoned.co.uk/lawexpress**

Acknowledgements

The authors would like to thank everyone who has been involved in the production of this book, but in particular Martina and Jesse for their support.

Claire de Than
Edwin Shorts

Publisher's acknowledgements

Our thanks go to all reviewers who contributed to the development of this text, including students who participated in research and focus groups which helped to shape the series format.

Introduction

Welcome to Law Express Human Rights! This vibrant and fast-developing subject is a very popular option on most LLB degrees, and is also usually taught as part of the compulsory Constitutional and Administrative law module. But that is only part of the picture: especially since the Human Rights Act came into force on 2 October 2000, almost every field of law has had to be measured against the standards of the European Convention on Human Rights, and there have been both expected and surprising changes to UK law as a result. The impact of the 1998 Act is immense and continuing, including a new role for judges and a new form of action for citizens who believe that their Convention rights have been violated by public authorities. However, common law and statute already protected some human rights within this jurisdiction, and so human rights law is a mesh of principles from a variety of sources, some of which have existed for a long period of time; it is important to appreciate how these principles fit together. In order to answer a question on any human rights topic, you will normally need to know the legal principles under English law and any relevant provisions of the European Convention on Human Rights, as well as how the latter is 'brought home' by the Human Rights Act. Chapters 1 and 2 are fundamental to your understanding of all other chapters, and you may need to combine the material in Chapters 1 and 2 with discussion of any of the rights and issues covered in the remaining chapters. In order to do well, you will also need to discuss those principles and relevant cases critically and analytically, and demonstrate your appreciation of relevant and topical contextual issues. Since this is a fascinating subject to study, students normally put in sufficient effort to pass, but in order to achieve good marks it is necessary to grapple with complex issues, a variety of different sources of law, quite a high level of uncertainty as to the scope of some specific rights and their future development, and the underlying theory of rights. Students who throw themselves into the task of attempting all of these things will be rewarded not only in their success in the subject but also through the greater appreciation and enjoyment they will gain from the subject. Students who do the bare minimum of work will, as in all law subjects, struggle to understand the principles or pass the examination!

It should go without saying that this book cannot be the basis of your study of human rights law; it must be used in the manner in which it was designed to be used, as an aid to revision of a subject which you have already studied. It cannot be a shortcut to avoid reading the cases/textbook/articles you were told to read by a lecturer, or to avoid attending classes. This book is a route map through the subject for revision purposes, with support and suggestions for the journey. We will show you how the principles and cases fit together, where the tensions in the law are, and remind you of the key points so that you can feel confident in your revision. If you are looking for a textbook in human rights law, then the same authors have written one of those too!

📖 REVISION NOTE

- The syllabus varies a great deal on different human rights law modules. Obviously, you need to know which rights are included in your syllabus before you start studying the course, let alone begin your revision! Some modules focus almost exclusively on the European Convention on Human Rights and the Human Rights Act. Others have a heavy element of police powers and public order under English law, plus the impact of the Human Rights Act. We have included the specific rights most commonly taught on LLB courses, but your course may include others, so do check. We have labelled chapters according to the manner in which rights are protected under English law, so you will need to 'translate' the chapter headings to fit your course if it looks at each ECHR right in turn. The material is covered here, but the order in your module might be different since there is no standard order in which to teach human rights law.

- It is always dangerous when revising law to miss out perceived 'topics' since this is one of the most common reasons for failure – lecturers have already done the topic-cutting for you. Such a strategy is particularly disastrous in human rights law, since many rights are balanced against others; one person's right to free speech must take account of another person's expectation of respect for his private life, for example. The ECHR and HRA interact and affect many fields of law, and their principles are relevant when looking at any specific human right. Examination questions often require discussion of more than one right, or comparison of the approach of English cases to that in Strasbourg, for example. You MUST know how ECHR cases and the HRA have impacted upon each of the human rights included on your individual syllabus.

- Read the cases. This is a subject where you need to make persuasive arguments, and judges are great inspiration for this.

- If there is time to do so before your exam and you have not already done so, read some academic articles to deepen your appreciation of the current debate in key areas of human rights law.

- Lecturers do not write this year's exam paper by looking at last year's; they write it on the basis of what has been taught this year, assuming that you have done the set reading. Although practising old exam questions is a valuable revision tool and builds your confidence, memorising the answers will ensure that you do badly in your exam.

- Keep up to date. This subject moves very fast indeed, and we are currently in uncertain times, with politicians and others clamouring for reform (and sometimes repeal) of the Human Rights Act. Read newspapers and incorporate current debates and new cases into your answers whenever they are relevant.

Before you begin, you can use the study plan available on the companion website to assess how well you know the material in this book and identify the areas where you may want to focus your revision.

Guided tour

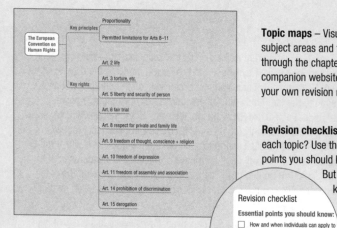

Topic maps – Visual guides highlight key subject areas and facilitate easy navigation through the chapter. Download them from the companion website to pin on your wall or add to your own revision notes.

Revision checklists – How well do you know each topic? Use these to identify essential points you should know for your exams. But don't panic if you don't know them all – the chapters will help you revise each point to ensure you are fully prepared. Print the checklists off the companion website and track your revision progress!

Revision checklist

Essential points you should know:

- [ ] How and when individuals can apply to t
- [ ] How 'the proportionality principle' operat
- [ ] The role of 'margin of appreciation'.
- [ ] The difference between absolute and li mately interfere with a right using par
- [ ] How States may derogate from the

Sample questions with Answer guidelines – Practice makes perfect! Read the question at the start of each chapter and consider how you would answer it. Guidance on structuring strong answers is provided at the end of the chapter. Try out additional sample questions online.

▮ Sample Question

Could you answer this question? Below is a typical essay question that could arise on this topic. Guidelines on answering the question are included at the end of this chapter, whilst a sample problem question and guidance on tackling it can be found on the companion website.

Assessment advice – Not sure how best to tackle a problem or essay question? Wondering what you may be asked? Use the assessment advice to identify the ways in which a subject may be examined and how to apply your knowledge effectively.

ASSESSMENT ADVICE

Essay Questions

Essay questions cover such issues as the way in which the court applies a margin of appreciation (see discussion below), the difference between absolute and limited rights and how derogation works. For example, in a question on the margin of appreciation, once you have outlined the way in which the court will take national differences into account when making its decision, you can demonstrate your wider understanding by examining and discussing the universality of human rights. Similarly, a question on derogation would require you to set out how a state may derogate from the Convention, and having done that, you should be able to discuss whether you think it is right that states can temporarily suspend human rights law.

Key definitions – Make sure you understand essential legal terms. Use the flashcards online to test your recall!

KEY DEFINITION: Margin of appreciation

The Convention recognises that the individual state is in a much better position to judge what laws are best suited for their citizens. Of course, problems arise due to the lack of uniformity between the domestic laws of member states. Accordingly, in order to deal

Key cases and Key statutes – Identify and review the important elements of the essential cases and statutes you will need to know for your exams.

> **KEY CASE**
>
> *Handyside v UK* (ECtHR)
>
> *Concerning: the margin of appreciation*
>
> Facts
>
> Handyside published a book entitled *The Little Red School Book* aimed at 12+, and which covered a range of issues including masturbation, orgasm and homosexuality. Copies of the book were seized and it was banned as an obscene publication. Handy-

> **KEY STATUTE**
>
> **ECHR Article 2: the right**
>
> Article 2 states that the r
> killed intentionally when
> is death (note that most
> Protocol 1 which outlaw

Make your answer stand out – This feature illustrates sources of further thinking and debate where you can maximise your marks. Use them to really impress your examiners!

> ✓ Make your answer stand out
>
> When answering an essay question on this topic, explain that the UK and Turkey have derogated from their responsibilities to deal with terrorism and consider detention periods for terrorist suspects under Article 5. This is discussed at more length in the Terrorism chapter, and a good discussion on when measures are strictly required by the exigencies of the situation is Lord Hoffmann's speech in *A v Secretary of State for the Home Department* (2005), and the Grand Chamber decision of *A and Others* v UK (2009).

Exam tips – Feeling the pressure? These boxes indicate how you can improve your exam performance when it really counts.

> **EXAM TIP**
>
> All of the Articles can come up as questions in their own right, but they will certainly come up as part of other questions. Understanding and explaining the particular Article/s and the relevant case law gives context to your answer in all of the areas explored later in this book.

Revision notes – Get guidance for effective revision. These boxes highlight related points and areas of overlap in the subject, or areas where your course might adopt a particular approach that you should check with your course tutor.

> **REVISION NOTE**
>
> Also see Discrimination chapter for a more detailed discussion of this particular Article.

Don't be tempted to . . . – This feature underlines areas where students most often trip up in exams. Use them to spot common pitfalls and avoid losing marks.

> ! Don't be tempted to . . .
>
> The ECHR and the HRA, are separate entities. Do not confuse them! Many students 'shoot themselves in the foot' by, referring to 'Article 8 of the Human Rights Act' in their answers, for example.

Read to impress – Focus on these carefully selected sources to extend your knowledge, deepen your understanding, and earn better marks in coursework as well as in exams.

> **READ TO IMPRESS**
>
> Baker, A. (2006) 'The enjoyment of rights and freedoms: a new conception of the "ambit" under Article 14', ECHR MLR, 69(5), 714–737.
>
> Berry, E. (2006) The extra territorial reach of the ECHR, EPL, 12(4), 629–55
>
> Palmer, S. (2006) A wrong turning: Article 3 ECHR and proportionality, CLJ, 65(2), 438–51.
>
> Weekes R. (2006) 'Focus on ECHR, Article 2', JR, 10(1), 19–26.

Glossary – Forgotten the meaning of a word? This quick reference covers key definitions and other useful terms.

Glossary of terms

The key definitions can be found within the chapter in which they occur as well as in the glossary below. These definitions are the essential terms that you must know and understand in order to prepare for an exam.

Guided tour of the companion website

Book resources are available to download. Print your own **topic maps** and **revision checklists**!

Use the **study plan** prior to your revision to help you assess how well you know the subject and determine which areas need most attention. Choose to take the full assessment or focus on targeted study units.

'Test your knowledge' of individual areas with quizzes tailored specifically to each chapter. **Sample problem and essay questions** are also available with guidance on crafting a good answer.

Flashcards help improve recall of important legal terms and key cases. Available in both electronic and printable formats

'You be the marker' gives you the chance to evaluate sample exam answers for different question types and understand how and why an examiner awards marks.

Download the **podcast** and listen as your own personal Law Express tutor guides you through a 10–15 minute audio session. You will be presented with a typical but challenging question and provided with a step-by-step explanation on how to approach the question, what essential elements your answer will need for a pass, how to structure a good response, and what to do to make your answer stand out so that you can earn extra marks.

All of this and more can be found when you visit **www.pearsoned.co.uk/lawexpress**

Table of cases and statutes

■ Cases

TABLE OF CASES AND STATUTES

■ Table of Statutes

Statutory Instruments

The Human Rights
Act 1998

Revision checklist

Essential points you should know:

☐ The main provisions of the HRA, the new mechanisms for the enforcement of human rights in the UK and how the Act's provisions have been applied in subsequent cases

☐ The relationship between the HRA and the European Convention on Human Rights

☐ The reasons why the 1998 Act was passed, the compromises which it represents and its constitutional significance

☐ The current debate about the Act, and potential reform

■ Topic map

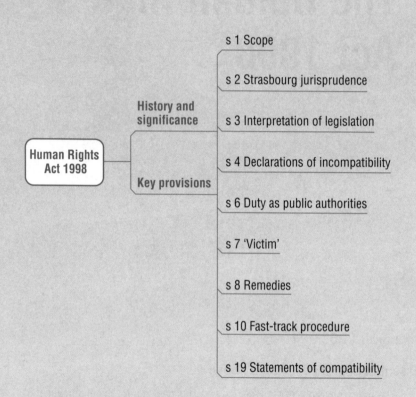

s 1 Scope

s 2 Strasbourg jurisprudence

History and significance

s 3 Interpretation of legislation

Human Rights Act 1998

s 4 Declarations of incompatibility

Key provisions

s 6 Duty as public authorities

s 7 'Victim'

s 8 Remedies

s 10 Fast-track procedure

s 19 Statements of compatibility

A printable version of this map is available from **ww.pearsoned.co.uk/lawexpress**

■ Introduction

The Human Rights Act 1998 came into force in October 2000, and was the culmination of a lengthy campaign to 'bring rights home' to the United Kingdom.

Until that date, citizens who wanted to enforce their ECHR rights could not do so in domestic courts, and faced a long and expensive process if they made an application to the Strasbourg court. The Human Rights Act is therefore a very significant piece of legislation, with far-reaching consequences for citizens, courts and public authorities. This topic is central to most human rights modules and is often examined, so it is important that you not only understand the provisions of the Act, but are also able to show how it has been applied in practice and to demonstrate a critical awareness of its provisions. You also need to be familiar with the political and historical context behind the Act, since its scope and effect reflect the compromises which were made in order to get it through Parliament; there were other possible forms which the Act could have taken. Hence you need to know what it does not do – it is not a Bill of Rights, it does not give judges the power to strike down legislation on grounds of incompatibility, and it does not fully incorporate the European Convention on Human Rights into domestic law. In recent years the Act has been subjected to much criticism, some of it ill-founded, and you should be aware of arguments both that it is too limited in its effect and that it goes too far in protecting some rights. In particular, make sure that you keep up to date with reform proposals – the Commission on a British Bill of Rights is reporting in 2012 and plenty has already been written about what it may or should recommend!

ASSESSMENT ADVICE

Essay questions

Essay questions on this topic generally require students to critique the Act's provisions and their application by judges in recent cases. In order to do this, you obviously need to have a detailed understanding of the Act's provisions and of key cases which apply them. However, it may be less obvious to you that you also need to be able to compare and contrast the position before and after the HRA came into force, including a discussion of key cases which showed the weaknesses in the prior position. Topical issues include the courts' powers under the Act, the extent to which there is 'horizontal effect' under the Act, the remedies available, the application of key concepts such as proportionality by domestic courts, the definition of 'public authority', and the extent to which domestic judges are free to depart

▶

from Strasbourg cases. Unfortunately, many students do badly on such questions because they seem only to be able to describe the main provisions of the Act rather than analyse and critique them, and many students do not show sufficient knowledge of recent cases or current debates about reform; this is a shame since a great deal has been written by academics on these issues. Another trap for the unwary or confused is to answer a question on the effect of the HRA by merely discussing the European Convention on Human Rights; as always, you need to answer the *precise* question on the examination paper, not a variant which you have prepared earlier or would have preferred to be asked! You need to be able to show that you understand the difference between the HRA and the ECHR; make sure that you know whether the question is asking you to address the ECHR, the HRA or both. It is also possible for a narrow type of question to be asked, perhaps the effect which the HRA is likely to have in a particular field such as freedom of expression or privacy; such questions require you to use material covered in those other topics, including relevant Strasbourg cases. You should be aware of such potential 'overlap' questions; revise this chapter in combination with Chapter 2.

Problem questions

Problem questions on this topic are frequently asked, and in essence will require much of the same knowledge as essay questions; the crucial point is that you must be able to *apply* that knowledge well to the facts of the question. Some questions will involve a hypothetical statute and expect you to assess whether and how its application to several named parties can be challenged under the HRA. Other questions may focus upon a particular right, such as freedom of assembly, or privacy, and so expect you to be able to apply key Strasbourg cases as well as those decided under the HRA. Make sure that you advise all the parties in the question, and look out for opportunities to demonstrate awareness of the strengths and weaknesses of the HRA and of recent cases (making sure of course that you do not stray away from the question or discuss irrelevant issues).

■ Sample question

Could you answer this question? Below is a typical essay question that could arise on this topic. Guidelines on answering the question are included at the end of this chapter, whilst a sample problem question and guidance on tackling it can be found on the companion website.

ESSAY QUESTION

To what extent has the HRA remedied the deficiencies in the recognition of human rights in the United Kingdom? Refer to recent domestic cases in your answer.

■ The prior position

You should, however, be careful not to make the mistake of believing that civil liberties and human rights were unprotected in UK law before 2 October 2000, and should be aware of the mechanisms which did protect them pre-HRA – some examiners like to set questions on this!

■ Overview of the HRA and its context

The most significant effect of the HRA is that it allows a citizen to rely upon Convention rights and freedoms directly in domestic courts for the first time. Other key features include that:

■ Strasbourg jurisprudence is now arguable in domestic courts, although not rendered binding upon UK judges;

■ public authorities (including courts) must not act incompatibly with Convention rights and freedoms;

■ UK legislation must, 'so far as it is possible to do so', be interpreted in a manner compatible with Convention rights and freedoms; if such an interpretation is not possible, then a declaration of incompatibility may be given or, in the case *only* of secondary legislation, it may be struck down;

■ judges may award remedies for breaches of the Convention.

The following table summarises the situation 'before and after' the HRA 1998 came into force on 2 October 2000.

Issue	Before 2/10/00	From 2/10/00
ECHR-incompatible statute	Courts could not set it aside or call its validity into question	Declaration of incompatibility possible or interpret it to render it compatible
ECHR-incompatible secondary/subordinate legislation	Court could only declare it unlawful if found it to be *ultra vires*, but could interpret it to render it compatible	Court can also strike it down, interpret it to render it compatible or declare it incompatible
Duty of courts in interpreting statutes	No duty to interpret in ECHR-friendly manner	Duty to interpret statutes 'so far as is possible' to comply with ECHR
Use of Strasbourg cases in domestic courts	Only in few limited situations	Duty on courts to take Strasbourg cases into account ▶

Issue	Before 2/10/00	From 2/10/00
Ability to argue ECHR rights and freedoms in domestic courts	No right to do so	Directly enforceable right to do so
Remedies for ECHR breaches	Take case to Strasbourg (after exhausting all domestic remedies and appeals)	Directly available in domestic courts
Grounds for challenging action by public authorities (state) which appears to infringe human rights	Judicial review for irrationality, illegality, breach of natural justice	Additional grounds based on compliance with ECHR
Effect of Convention-violating actions by public authorities	Lawful (unless illegal on other grounds)	Unlawful in their own right

■ Key provisions of the HRA

We shall look at each of the main provisions of the Act in turn, evaluating their effect and referring to important cases along the way.

KEY STATUTE

HRA 1998, s 1

This defines the ECHR rights which are being 'given further effect' by the HRA 1998. Note that the list of Convention rights given effect in the United Kingdom omits Arts 1 and 13 of the Convention, and that s 1(2) allows further limitations to be made by derogations and reservations.

KEY CASE

Re McKerr [2004] 1 WLR 807 (HL)

Concerning: distinction between the ECHR and HRA 1998; non-retroactivity of the HRA

Facts

Gervaise McKerr was shot dead by the RUC in 1982. His son brought domestic proceedings arguing a breach of Art. 2, also contending that there was a common law equivalent of the Art. 2 right to an effective investigation into the death.

Legal principle

The House of Lords held that the HRA could not apply since it had not been in force at the time of the death, and further that there was no equivalent common law right to Art. 2. The judges made some useful statements about the distinction between the ECHR and the HRA. Lord Nicholls stated that the two sets of rights exist side by side, but that there are significant differences between them; ECHR rights are not part of domestic law, but the HRA rights are, and the latter are subject to interpretation by domestic courts.

KEY STATUTE

HRA 1998, s 2

Domestic courts must 'take into account' the prior decisions of the ECtHR (and of the now disbanded Commission) where they are relevant, but they are not obliged to follow them. Courts have differed in their interpretation of the extent of the obligation imposed by 'taking into account'.

In *R (on the application of Alconbury Ltd)* v *Secretary of State for the Environment* (2001) judges had to interpret s 2 HRA 1998. Lord Slynn stated that (at 26) 'In the absence of some special circumstances it seems to me that the court should follow any clear and constant jurisprudence of the ECtHR' since to do otherwise would be likely to result in the case going to that court. However, also see Lord Hoffmann who confirms that ECHR cases are merely persuasive (at 76): 'The House is not bound by the decisions of the European Court and, if I thought that the Divisional Court was right to hold that they compelled a conclusion fundamentally at odds with the distribution of powers under the British constitution, I would have considerable doubt as to whether they should be followed.' In *Kay* v *Lambeth* (2006) the House of Lords unanimously confirmed that the HRA 1998 does not change the rules of precedent in domestic courts. Hence, where the Court of Appeal had found a conflict between a HL decision and a subsequent ECtHR decision, it should apply the precedent from the HL and give leave to appeal to the Lords. It is only where there is a strongly arguable case that the domestic precedent is incompatible with the Convention that such a precedent should not be followed.

 Make your answer stand out

Exactly *how* and *when* judges should 'take into account' Strasbourg cases has become a hot topic, and familiarity with recent cases on that issue will elevate the quality of an exam answer. Several Supreme Court or House of Lords cases are relevant here: *Re P and Others* (2009) 1 AC 173 (unmarried couples and adoption) *Doherty* v *Birmingham City* ▶

Council (2009) 1 AC 367 (evicting travellers), *R* v *Horncastle* (2010) 2 AC 373 (admissibility of evidence), *R (Purdy)* v *DPP* (2010) 1 AC 345 (right to die), *AF* v *Secretary of State for the Home Department* (2009) (control orders). What reasons did the court give in each case to justify its decision as to whether it could and should depart from prior relevant Strasbourg authority? Is there a clear rule?

KEY STATUTE

HRA 1998, s 3

According to s 3, 'so far as is possible', domestic primary and secondary legislation should be read and given effect in a manner which is compatible with Convention rights. Thus, legislation may be reinterpreted in order to render it rights-compliant. This is a major change from the pre-HRA position, where courts could only use the Convention to interpret *ambiguous* legislation.

Section 3 has proved to be one of the most important provisions of the HRA 1998, and has led to some high-profile and difficult decisions for judges, as well as some rational reinterpretation and modernisation of older statutes. An important issue is the extent to which it is 'possible' to reinterpret the clear words of a statute rather than issuing a declaration of incompatibility under s 4 HRA.

KEY CASE

R v *A* [2002] 1 AC 45 (HL)

Concerning: admissibility of evidence of rape complainant's previous sexual behaviour; interpretation of s 41, Youth Justice and Criminal Evidence Act 1999; courts' duties under s 3, HRA 1998

Facts

Re s 41, the House of Lords held that if evidence of a relationship between D and V were not heard in court, then there could be a violation of the defendant's right to a fair trial. Section 41 could in some cases prevent the defendant from putting forward a full defence.

Legal principle

Courts should use their powers under s 3 HRA to interpret s 41 of the YJCEA 1999. The result would be that courts could admit evidence of the complainant's previous sexual history whenever they considered it necessary to ensure a fair trial. Section 3 places a duty on courts to strive to find a possible interpretation which is compatible with Convention rights. A declaration of incompatibility should be a last resort.

The effect of *R* v *A* was that a declaration of incompatibility was avoided, but also that s 41's purpose is now only partially achieved. Lord Hope, dissenting, could not interpret s 41 in the manner chosen by the majority, since to do so was judicial legislation rather than a 'possible' interpretation of s 41. In his view, the majority's approach was a clear contradiction of Parliamentary intention; if there was a problem with Art. 6, a declaration of incompatibility should have been issued.

KEY CASE

Bellinger v *Bellinger* [2003] 2 AC 467 (HL)

Concerning: the scope and use of courts' powers under s 3, HRA 1998; the interpretation of 'man and woman' in s 11, Matrimonial Causes Act 1973

Facts

Section 11 of the Matrimonial Causes Act 1973 made marriages void in certain situations, including where the parties to the marriage were not a man and a woman. The claimant was a transsexual woman who went through a marriage ceremony with a man in 1981, and wanted legal recognition of that marriage. The House of Lords held that the marriage was not valid since English law did not recognise a change of gender.

Legal principle

It was not possible for the court to use its s 3, HRA powers to interpret 'man and woman' in the 1973 Act to include a person who had undergone gender reassignment surgery. However, a Declaration of Incompatibility was issued for s 11(c) of the Matrimonial Causes Act since it was incompatible with the rights protected by Arts 8 and 12, ECHR. The Gender Recognition Act 2004 was then passed in order to remove the incompatibility.

Note that in *Ghaidan* v *Mendoza* (2004) the majority of the House of Lords did manage to interpret the word 'spouse' in the Rent Act 1977 to include a same-sex partner, and the words 'living together as man and wife' as 'living together as if man and wife'. Lord Millett, dissenting, thought it should be left to Parliament to change the law in this manner since it was clearly not a statute intended to protect same-sex partnerships.

 Make your answer stand out

There has been a great deal of academic debate about the 'proper' use of s 3: refer to Kavanagh, A. (2005) 'Unlocking the Human Rights Act': The 'Radical' Approach to s 3(1)', EHRLR 260; Nicol, D. (2004) 'Statutory interpretation and human rights after Anderson' PL 274.

KEY STATUTE

HRA 1998, s 4

Section 4 gives courts the power to issue a declaration of incompatibility when they determine that a statutory provision is incompatible with a Convention right.

! Don't be tempted to . . .

It is important to understand the relationship between ss 3 and 4. Section 3 imposes a *duty* on courts whereas s 4 only gives them a *power.* Does this explain the courts' apparent preference for Convention-compliant interpretation by reading in words or phrases to statutes, leaving declarations of incompatibility as a last resort? Consider the results achieved in the cases discussed above under s 3 and in *Hammond* v *Secretary of State for the Home Department* (2005), *Secretary of State for the Home Department* v *MB* (2007) and *A* v *Secretary of State for the Home Department* (2005) – is any consistent policy evident as to whether and when s 3 or s 4 will be used to 'cure' incompatibility? Are courts going beyond their HRA role in reinterpreting legislation when the result conflicts with Parliament's purpose?

The aim of s 4 is to preserve Parliamentary sovereignty – courts cannot overrule primary legislation, they can only issue a declaration of incompatibility and wait for Parliament to fix the problem; the offending legislation remains in force and must be applied by courts until then. In practice, Parliament has not refused to amend legislation once a declaration of incompatibility has been issued.

KEY CASE

Bellinger v *Bellinger* [2003] 2 AC 467 (HL)

Concerning: declaration of incompatibility under s 4, HRA 1998; the relationship between ss 3 and 4 of the HRA

Facts

Mrs Bellinger's alternative claim was that, if the House of Lords was unable to use its s 3 interpretative powers to render the statutory provision compliant with her rights under Arts 8 and 12 of the ECHR, then it should issue a declaration of incompatibility under s 4.

Legal principle

The House of Lords issued a declaration of incompatibility. It was clear from Strasbourg cases, including *Goodwin* v *UK* (2002), that the statute in question was incompatible with Mrs Bellinger's ECHR rights. Since s 3 of the HRA did not give courts the power to legislate, s 4 should be used; the matter was one for Parliament. 'Robust interpretation' was allowed under s 3, but not judicial legislation. Various supporting reasons were given for this decision, including that recognition of gender reassignment would affect many fields of English law and the necessary changes should not be made piecemeal.

EXAM TIP

You should be aware of a range of cases where courts have discussed whether a declaration of incompatibility should be issued, and the result in each case (including the reasons given by the court for their decision). This will help you when dealing with the important issue mentioned above, i.e. when courts should use their s 3 powers and when they should apply s 4. *R* v *A* (2002) (above), *R* v *Shayler* (2002) and *A* v *Secretary of State for the Home Department* (2004) are helpful in this respect.

So, the courts' powers and duties when faced with potentially HRA-incompatible legislation can be summarised as follows.

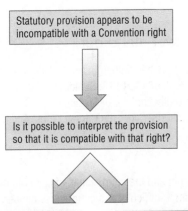

KEY STATUTE

HRA 1998, s 6

Section 6(1) makes it unlawful for a **public authority** to act in a manner which is incompatible with Convention rights, unless its actions are authorised by primary legislation. The definition of 'public authority' is thus a crucial one and has proved difficult in practice.

KEY DEFINITION: Public Authority

A body whose functions are public (expressly including courts and tribunals), or whose functions are partly public in nature. Where a body's functions are only partly public in nature, then it is only bound by s 6 in respect of its public functions.

! Don't be tempted to . . .

Don't neglect the definition of public authority and public functions. The HRA does not give a full definition of these terms, and so it has been left to judges to shape one of the most important concepts in the Act. If a body is a public authority, then the Act gives individuals direct remedies for Convention-breaching acts by that body. Cases on the meaning of these terms are therefore very important, and the division between public and private actions has been controversial.

✓ Make your answer stand out

On the issue of the scope of 'public authority' see McDermott, M. (2003) 'The elusive nature of the public function', 66 MLR 113; Sunkin, M. (2004) 'Pushing forward the frontiers of human rights protection', PL 643; Joint committee on Human Rights (2007) 'The meaning of public authority under the Human Rights Act'. Refer to them in exam answers where relevant.

While government departments and the courts clearly fall within the scope of s 6 as public authorities, there has been more difficulty and controversy concerning the classification of bodies which have both private and public functions. The issue first reached the HL in *Aston Cantlow PCC* v *Wallbank* (2003) where the House held that the Parochial Church Council was not a public authority within s 6 since it was essentially a self-governing religious organisation which did not exercise delegated state powers; its functions were not public. In *R (Heather)* v *Leonard Cheshire Foundation* (2002), a housing organisation which had closed a care home was held not to be a public authority and not to have a public law function within the scope of s 6, even though it was publicly funded, fulfilled a role which would otherwise have had to be filled by the state, and was subject to state regulation. The same result was achieved in *R (Johnson)* v *Havering LBC* (2008), as below.

KEY CASE

R (Johnson) v Havering LBC and YL v Birmingham City Council [2008] 1 AC 95 (HL)

Concerning: definition of 'public authority' for s 6, HRA; bodies with partly private and partly public functions, or which perform functions which would otherwise fall to the state

Facts

In *Johnson*, residents of local authority care homes were challenging the decision that the homes should be transferred to the private sector, since they argued that this would deprive them of protection for their human rights. In *YL*, an 84-year-old woman with Alzheimer's challenged the decision of a private care home to evict her, arguing that this was a breach of her rights under Arts 2, 3 and 8, ECHR.

Legal principle

Lord Bingham and Baroness Hale dissenting, the House of Lords dismissed the appeals and held that a private care home, under contract with a local authority, was not performing a public function within the meaning of s 6 and so residents could not bring actions against the home for breach of their Convention rights. Section 6 identifies two types of public authority: 'core' public authorities which have only public functions and 'hybrid' bodies which have both private and public functions. Hybrid authorities are only to be regarded as public authorities when the particular act in question is by nature 'public'. Provision of care or accommodation for those unable to arrange it for themselves is not an inherently governmental function (per Lord Mance). Thus, courts are emphasising not only the nature of the body as public or private but also the nature of the function which has brought the body before them. As always, it is worth knowing the reasons behind the dissenting judgments.

✎ EXAM TIP

How much 'horizontal effect' does s 6 HRA create?

This could equally have been a Revision note or a Make your answer stand out! An issue which has caused a great deal of academic debate is whether and to what extent the HRA creates rights between individuals (horizontal rights) rather than between an individual and the state (vertical rights). Since it is unlawful for a court to deny individuals their Convention rights, the potential is there for the common law to be developed by judges so that it becomes Convention-compliant, resulting in Convention rights becoming enforceable by individuals against individuals in domestic courts. A topical example of 'horizontal effect' for the HRA is privacy, where cases such as *Douglas* v *Hello!* (2001), *Campbell* v *Mirror* ▶

Group (2004), *McKennitt* v *Ash* (2007), *Murray* v *Big Pictures* (2008) and *Mosley* v *News of the World* (2008) appear to have brought domestic law into line with the ECtHR decision in *Von Hannover* v *Germany* (2005). Note, however, the House of Lords statement in *Wainwright* v *Home Office* (2004) that what had happened in cases such as *Douglas* was merely an expansion of the law of confidentiality, not the creation of a new privacy right. At the time of writing, we were eagerly awaiting the decision in *Von Hannover* v *Germany* (2011) – has it been reported by the time you are reading this, and what did the Court hold? When revising this issue, remember to cross-reference with Chapter 6 of this book (which deals with privacy under English law) and the discussion of Article 8 in Chapter 2.

 Make your answer stand out

When discussing the creation of horizontal effect, refer to e.g. Phillipson, G. (2007) 'Clarity postponed: horizontal effect after Campbell' in Fenwick, H. Phillipson G. and Masterman, R. *Judicial reasoning under the UK Human Rights Act*. Cambridge: Cambridge University Press.

KEY STATUTE

HRA 1998, s 7

Section 7 imposes limits upon the ability to bring a free-standing HRA action to court or to argue a Convention right as a defence; a litigant must be a victim of the alleged unlawful act before he can do either. This requirement is more restrictive than the usual rules of judicial review, which require the applicant to have a 'sufficient interest' in the matter to be reviewed. However, s 7(7) requires domestic courts to 'apply' Strasbourg cases on the issue of who is a victim, not simply to take them into account. This is important since the Strasbourg court has construed 'victim' widely to include potential victims. A free-standing HRA case must be brought within the s 7(5) time limit of one year, in contrast to the usual judicial review time limit of three months.

The House of Lords in *Rushbridger* v *Attorney-General and DPP* (2004) held that a declaration of incompatibility can only be issued where the claimant is personally affected by the provision in question, or there is a risk that it will impact on his rights.

KEY STATUTE

HRA 1998, s 8

Section 8 provides that a court may 'grant such relief or remedy, or make such order, within its powers as it considers just and appropriate' – in other words each court has its full range of usual remedies to apply in a case argued under the HRA. This includes injunctions and damages.

HRA 1998, s 10

This section creates the 'fast track procedure': after a declaration of incompatibility has been issued or a Strasbourg decision has stated that a domestic provision is incompatible with the Convention, then a Minister may amend the offending provision(s) via delegated legislation. This procedure is controversial since it allows the normal Parliamentary procedures to be avoided, but under s 10 'compelling reasons' must exist for using a fast-track procedure rather than primary legislation.

HRA 1998, s 19

Before the Second Reading of a Bill, a Minister must make a written statement as to whether it is compatible with the Convention rights. It is difficult to assess the constitutional significance of such statements.

A statement of incompatibility was given in respect of s 321(2) of the Communications Act 2003; the relevant Minister stated that the government would proceed with the Bill in spite of not having made a statement of compatibility. Section 321(2) makes political advertising unlawful and appears to conflict with the decision of the ECtHR in *VgT* v *Switzerland* (2001). But in *R (Animal Defenders International)* v *Secretary of State for Culture, Media and Sport* (2008) the court found that the ban on political advertising did not violate freedom of expression under Art. 10 since there are strong reasons justifying political impartiality in the broadcasting mass media. Of course, a challenge to s 321(2) could still be made in Strasbourg.

■ Putting it all together

Answer guidelines

See the essay question at the start of the chapter.

Approaching the question

This question requires a 'before and after HRA' comparison of the enforcement of human rights in the UK. It is crucial that you *do* refer to recent English cases in your answer; there is no way out of it! You need to be able to explain and critically assess the traditional methods of upholding human rights under the common law pre-October 2000, as well as the mechanisms for enforcing Convention rights under the HRA. You could refresh your memory by looking at the 'before and after' table at the beginning of this chapter.

Important points to include

■ Although pre-HRA there was no constitutional Bill of Rights or direct mechanism by which an individual could bring an ECHR claim in a domestic court, there was protection under the common law for fundamental rights and freedoms, including the right to a fair trial and the doctrine of *ultra vires* which curbed governmental excesses that infringed individual rights, and judicial creativity upheld some rights or defences, e.g. qualified privilege. Various statutes also created express rights, such as those of suspects under the Police and Criminal Evidence Act 1984.

■ However, the general position pre-HRA was one where it was difficult for citizens to enforce their ECHR rights without taking the long and expensive route to Strasbourg. Courts could not apply Convention rights directly unless they were within the narrow exceptions in *R* v *Secretary of State for the Home Department ex p Brind* (1991). The UK in general had a poor record in Strasbourg for upholding the Convention rights within its jurisdiction.

■ You should explain and assess the mechanisms introduced by the HRA 1998 and the contrast between these and the prior position. This would be a good place in which to refer to those 'recent cases' while discussing ss 2, 3, 4 and 6. The HRA provides remedies in domestic courts for ECHR breaches, and this is an important change. However, there are still criticisms possible of each of these sections and of the overall effect of the Act, and you should be aware of these.

 Make your answer stand out

Average answers tend to be very enthusiastic about the changes introduced by the HRA, miss the point that there was protection for human rights under the 'old' law and lack specific references to cases. A good answer would demonstrate understanding of the academic debate about the significance of the HRA and detailed knowledge of plenty of recent relevant cases. This should be no problem at all in such a dynamic and fast-moving subject; there are plenty of articles and cases to choose from. You could also show that you know about cases where the UK's protection of Convention rights was found lacking pre-HRA, e.g. *Sunday Times* v *UK* (1979), *Malone* v *UK* (1984); and, indeed after the HRA, e.g. *Wainwright* v *UK* (2007). You could also explore the argument that the HRA only seems to be ensuring Convention-compliance so far, not going beyond existing ECHR rights.

READ TO IMPRESS

Klug, F. (2007) 'A Bill of Rights: do we need one or do we already have one?', PL 701.

Leigh, I. and Masterman, R. (2007) *Making rights real: enforcing the Human Rights Act.* Oxford: Hart.

Phillipson, G. (2007) 'Clarity postponed: horizontal effect after Campbell', in Fenwick, H. Phillipson, G. and Masterman, R. *Judicial reasoning under the UK Human Rights Act.* Cambridge: Cambridge University Press.

Straw, J. (2010) 'The Human Rights Act ten years on', EHRLR 576.

www.pearsoned.co.uk/lawexpress

 Go online to access more revision support including quizzes to test your knowledge, sample questions with answer guidelines, podcasts you can download, and more!

The European Convention on Human Rights

2

Revision checklist

Essential points you should know:

- [ ] How and when individuals can apply to the European Court on Human Rights
- [ ] How 'the proportionality principle' operates.
- [ ] The role of 'margin of appreciation'.
- [ ] The difference between absolute and limited rights; and how a State can legitimately interfere with a right using Paragraph 2 of Articles 8, 9,10 or 11.
- [ ] How States may derogate from the Convention.

■ Topic Map

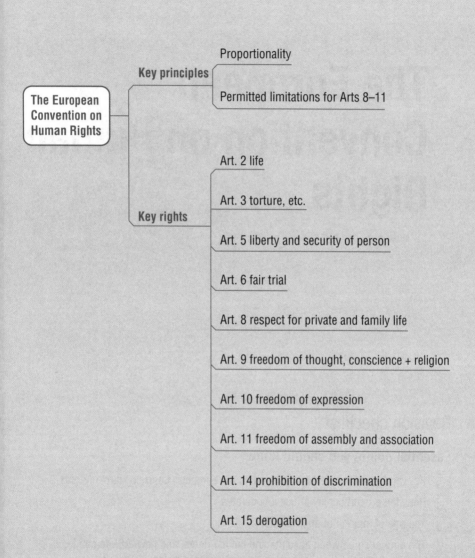

The European Convention on Human Rights

Key principles
- Proportionality
- Permitted limitations for Arts 8–11

Key rights
- Art. 2 life
- Art. 3 torture, etc.
- Art. 5 liberty and security of person
- Art. 6 fair trial
- Art. 8 respect for private and family life
- Art. 9 freedom of thought, conscience + religion
- Art. 10 freedom of expression
- Art. 11 freedom of assembly and association
- Art. 14 prohibition of discrimination
- Art. 15 derogation

A printable version of this topic map is available from **www.pearsoned.co.uk/lawexpress**

■ Introduction

The European Convention on Human Rights provides the framework for the protection of civil liberties and human rights across Europe.

Understanding of the European Convention on Human Rights (ECHR or the Convention) is absolutely central to an understanding of civil liberties and human rights in the UK. The Convention has affected all areas of UK law, and so every question you answer in your exam needs to have a reference to the ECHR and the relevant Article or Articles. You should also know how, when and why the Convention was created and how it is enforced.

There are two methods under which rights can be enforced in the EctHR:

- state v state;
- individual v state.

Both are provided for in Article 34, but the second is far more common.

When answering an essay question on this topic you should note that the UK and Turkey have derogated from their responsibilities to deal with terrorism.

ASSESSMENT ADVICE

Essay Questions

Essay questions cover such issues as the way in which the court applies a margin of appreciation (see discussion below), the difference between absolute and limited rights and how derogation works. For example, in a question on the margin of appreciation, once you have outlined the way in which the court will take national differences into account when making its decision, you can demonstrate your wider understanding by examining and discussing the universality of human rights. Similarly, a question on derogation would require you to set out how a state may derogate from the Convention, and having done that, you should be able to discuss whether you think it is right that states can temporarily suspend human rights law.

Problem Questions

Problem questions are becoming more and more the norm on this topic. A possible problem question might ask you to examine which Articles have been breached in a particular scenario, and work out what legal avenues the individual in the scenario might explore. In this case you will need a sound grasp of the extent of each of the main Articles, and you will need to understand how to apply to the court in Strasbourg.

■ Sample Question

Could you answer this question? Below is a typical essay question that could arise on this topic. Guidelines on answering the question are included at the end of this chapter, whilst a sample problem question and guidance on tackling it can be found on the companion website.

> **ESSAY QUESTION**
>
> Once a state has signed up to the ECHR they can never act in such a way as to interfere with the human rights of an individual. Discuss.

■ Fundamental ECHR Principles

> **!** Don't be tempted to . . .
>
> The ECHR and the HRA, are separate entities. Do not confuse them! Many students 'shoot themselves in the foot' by, referring to 'Article 8 of the Human Rights Act' in their answers, for example.

'Necessary in a democratic society'

When dealing with the issue of whether an interference was justified as being 'necessary in a democratic society', it is essential to examine whether or not a fair balance has been maintained between two competing interests; the right protected in the respective Article, andthe general interests of society via the legitimate aims as specified in Articles 8–11. The concept of 'necessity' requires the court to decide whether the 'interference' complained of corresponded to a 'pressing social need', whether it was '**proportionate** to the legitimate aim pursued', whether the reasons given by the national authorities to justify it are 'relevant and sufficient'.

> **KEY DEFINITION: Proportionality**
>
> Understanding proportionality is essential to an understanding of the ECHR. Some rights in the Convention allow interference by the state. The principle of proportionality requires, firstly, that any interference with a Convention right or freedom must not be disproportionate to the legitimate aim which the state argues for the interference; and secondly, proportionality deals primarily with deciding where a particular balance lies; the balance

being between safeguarding the fundamental rights of the individual with those interests of society as a whole. Proportionality is a tool that the court uses to balance the competing interests in the particular situation before them. It is especially important when dealing with Articles 8–11, but is by no means restricted to those particular provisions. On the other hand, you should also be aware that not all ECHR rights have a proportionality analysis; most obviously, Article 3 can never be interfered with, so no balancing exercise can be carried out to consider whether the torture or other breach is lawful.

In essence, the court considers whether the exercise of the power of the state could have been carried out in a way which interferes less with the exercise of the rights of the individual. If the same result could have been achieved with less interference, the measures the state took will be disproportionate and therefore will breach the Convention.

KEY DEFINITION: Margin of appreciation

The Convention recognises that the individual state is in a much better position to judge what laws are best suited for their citizens. Of course, problems arise due to the lack of uniformity between the domestic laws of member states. Accordingly, in order to deal with cultural and legal diversity across the signatory states, the EctHR has developed the concept of a 'margin of appreciation'. Thus, in certain circumstances, you should be aware that states may be given a degree of flexibility when the court has to decide whether or not the measures taken by the authorities were justified. A good example of the margin of appreciation in action is the case of *Handyside*.

KEY CASE

Handyside v *UK* (1976) (ECtHR)

Concerning: the margin of appreciation

Facts

Handyside published a book entitled *The Little Red School Book* aimed at 12+, and which covered a range of issues including masturbation, orgasm and homosexuality. Copies of the book were seized and it was banned as an obscene publication. Handyside then brought a case against the UK arguing that this was a breach of the right to free expression under Article 10 of the ECHR. The UK government argued that the interference was legitimate because the action was aimed at protecting morals.

Legal principle

As well as discussing the questions of being prescribed by law, meeting a legitimate objective and being necessary in a democratic society (see below for more on these ▶

issues), the EctHR outlined the importance of allowing states a margin of appreciation. Mr Handyside argued that the fact that the book was being published across Europe and had not been banned anywhere else meant that it must be allowed to be published in the UK, but the court held that each state can have regard to the different views in their society about the protection of morals.

Each of the key rights will now be examined in turn. This chapter only considers the most commonly used Articles, and knowing these Articles is fundamental to answering questions on the rest of the areas covered in a human rights/civil liberties module.

✎ EXAM TIP

All of the Articles can come up as questions in their own right, but they will certainly come up as part of other questions. Understanding and explaining the particular Article/s and the relevant case law gives context to your answer in all of the areas explored later in this book.

When you are revising these Articles, make sure you are clear on the content of the Article and the key cases which have explored the extent of the Article. Also think about and apply the specific topics later in the book – if the question asks you to consider the right to freedom of expression in Article 10, you can use your knowledge of public order and contempt of court to give your answer more depth.

KEY STATUTE

ECHR Article 2: the right to life

Article 2 states that the right to life shall be protected by law and individuals can only be killed intentionally when a court orders it following a conviction and the penalty in law is death (note that most member states have now signed up to the additional rights in Protocol 1 which outlaws the death penalty altogether).

This right is not breached if the state uses no more force than absolutely necessary, (1) in defence of any person from unlawful violence; (2) in order to effect a lawful arrest or to prevent the escape of a person lawfully detained; or (3) in action lawfully taken for the purpose of quelling a riot or insurrection.

Although at first glance this Article appears very simple, there are a few aspects of it which you should note. Bear in mind that issues such as a right to die, euthanasia and assisted suicide have no direct application to this Article (see *R (Pretty) v DPP* (2001) in the House of Lords and *Pretty v UK* (2002) in the EctHR). However, it does include a positive duty to

protect the right to life (see the case of *Osman* discussed below) and to i
state has used force which has resulted in death or where a state has fai
(see *McCann* v *UK* (1995)).

Exceptions to continual state protection

Continual state protection for an individual, over an indefinite period, may prove to be unrealistic, however much required. For instance, in *X* v *Ireland* (1973) the applicant, for three and a half years received full police protection from attempts on his life by the IRA. Once this protection stopped, he alleged that this amounted to a breach of Article 2. The Commission formed the opinion that there was no duty on the state to provide unlimited protection of this kind (in this case, it could have amounted to a permanent bodyguard), therefore there was no violation. The exceptions under Article 2 will only apply where the use of force is absolutely necessary, which means that the force used must be strictly proportionate to the achievement of the permitted purpose, and the only permitted purposes are those listed in Article 2(2)(a)–(c) (see *Kelly* v *UK* and *Stewart* v *UK* (2001) in which the actions of the police in Northern Ireland were closely examined by the Court). The main right to life issues in the United Kingdom involve the following: euthanasia; pregnancy terminations and the rights of the unborn child; deaths in detention; withdrawal of medical treatment and finally, the investigation of deaths.

KEY CASE

Osman v *UK* (2000) 29 EHRR 245 (ECtHR)

Concerning: the duty of the state to protect the right to life

Facts

After a teacher became obsessed with their son, the Osman family informed the police and asked for their assistance. After repeated incidents, and no effective police action, the teacher broke into the family home, seriously injured the son and murdered the father.

Legal principle

A state breaches Article 2 where the state authorities know or ought to have known that there was a real and immediate risk to life and yet fail to take measures within their power to avoid the risk. However, in this particular case, the court held that there was no breach of this positive aspect of Article 2 because the previous incidents were not life-threatening; there was no proof it was the former teacher and there was no evidence that the teacher was prone to violence prior to his attack.

However, where the circumstances dictate that the police should have acted to prevent loss of life due to the existing known threat and did not do so, then the state will be held liable

...mission, e.g. *Kontrova* v *Slovakia* (2007). A less obvious protection under Article 2 ...des undertakings by the state authorities to effectively investigate potential unlawful acts against individuals. It was stated in *Bubbins* v *UK* (2005) that the 'investigation should be independent, accessible to the victim's family, carried out with reasonable promptness and expedition, effective in the sense that it is capable of leading to a determination of whether the force used in such cases was or was not justified in the circumstances or otherwise unlawful, and afford a sufficient element of public scrutiny of the investigation or its results' (at para 137). See *Hugh Jordan* v *UK* (2002) where the Court said that the degree of public scrutiny required may well vary from case to case. However, it was vital the next-of-kin of the victim be involved in the procedure to the extent necessary to safeguard his or her legitimate interests, in order to avoid possible state irregularity. See also *Ramsahai and Others* v *Netherlands* (2007).

KEY STATUTE

ECHR Article 3: the prohibition of torture

No one shall be subject to torture or to inhuman or degrading treatment or punishment.

Torture may be defined as the deliberate inhuman treatment or punishment causing very serious and cruel suffering. Note that there are no exceptions to Article 3, which means that torture or inhuman or degrading treatment or punishment can never be justified. States have a positive obligation to prevent anyone from suffering a breach of Article 3:

Case	Scenario
Soering v *UK* (1989)	Sending Soering back to the USA where there was a chance he would be put on death row was not permitted because waiting on death row would constitute a breach of Article 3.
Chahal v *UK* (1997)	The UK could not deport Chahal where there was a substantial risk of being subjected to torture if returned.
D v *UK* (1997)	D, a citizen of St Kitts, was imprisoned in the UK for drugs offences. Whilst in prison he was diagnosed with HIV and was given treatment for the condition. At the end of his sentence, he was to be deported but he appealed against this action on compassionate grounds because he would not be able to get medical treatment in St Kitts. It was held that, due to the *exceptional circumstances*, any action by the UK government to deport D from the United Kingdom to St Kitts would constitute a breach of Article 3. This was because he would be exposed to a real risk of dying in distressing circumstances due to a lack of adequate medical treatment or other support and the additional significant risk of further infection.

Case	Scenario
N v Secretary of State for the Home Department (2005)	The House of Lords considered D, but held that N's advanced HIV was not sufficient to prevent deportation because her circumstances were not sufficiently 'exceptional', partly because she could still get treatment in her native Uganda, albeit at considerable cost to herself. In 2008 the Grand Chamber (*N v UK* (2008)) heard her case and made the following clarifications:

(1) An individual cannot escape deportation solely for the reason that s/he is able to benefit from the medical treatment and care in the host state.

(2) Merely because life expectancy would be reduced, if deported, is not *per se* a satisfactory reason for refusing expulsion.

(3) Even though there is a definite question under Article 3, i.e., whether to remove or not, if the medical facilities in the receiving state are inferior, it would only be 'in a very exceptional case, where the humanitarian grounds against the removal are compelling'.

Recognise the distinction between the different forms of ill-treatment

In order to qualify an act as torture, a distinction must be made between that type of ill-treatment with that of inhuman or degrading treatment or punishment. For example, 'inhuman' include instances where it was premeditated, was applied for hours at a stretch and caused either actual bodily injury or intense physical and mental suffering. 'Degrading' includes instances where the treatment humiliates or debases an individual, showing a lack of respect for, or diminishing, his or her human dignity, or arouses feelings of fear, anguish or inferiority capable of breaking an individual's moral and physical resistance. You should also bear in mind that physical injury is not necessary – merely the threat of ill-treatment may, under certain circumstances, constitute a violation of Article 3. See, for example, *Gafgen v Germany* (2011).

KEY CASE

Ireland v *UK* (1978) 2 EHRR 25 (ECtHR)

Concerning: Article 3

Facts

Ireland brought a case under Article 34 ECHR (state v state) alleging that the UK's treatment of IRA detainees breached Article 3. The detainees were subjected to the so-called

▶

'five techniques' of interrogation, which included sleep deprivation, standing spread-eagled against a wall for hours, hooding, and food and drink deprivation. Ireland argued that these techniques amounted to torture under Article 3.

Legal principle

The court held that Article 3 creates a sliding scale, in which torture and inhuman and degrading treatment and punishment were distinguished by the difference of intensity in the suffering of the detainees. The treatment of the prisoners did amount to inhuman and degrading treatment, but was not sufficiently serious to constitute torture.

■ Article 5: the right to liberty and security

Article 5 states that everyone has the right to liberty and security of person. The right is about actual deprivation of liberty not mere restriction of liberty or movement, but the court has held that the difference is one of fact and degree, not nature or substance.

In other words, there is a sliding scale and Article 5 is engaged somewhere along that scale, when all of the factors in the situation add up to a deprivation of liberty, not just a restriction of movement.

The whole essence of Article 5(1) is that any arrest or detention must be lawful and 'in accordance with a procedure prescribed by law'. This was first explained by the EctHR in *Guzzardi* v *Italy* (1980); see more discussion in Police powers and Terrorism chapters in relation to police stop and search powers (in particular *R (on the application of Gillan)* v *Commissioner of Police of the Metropolis* (2006) in the Terrorism chapter).

This right may only be overridden in certain circumstances where the procedure is laid down by law, and the list in Article 5 is exhaustive. These situations include:

■ Detention after conviction by a court and a lawful arrest following a reasonable suspicion of criminal activity. The *reasonableness of the suspicion* will be judged on the facts of the individual case whatever the law allowing detention states is the standard required (see *Guzzardi* v *Italy* (1980). In *Fox, Campbell and Hartley* v *UK* (1990) the court said that reasonable suspicion infers the existence of facts or information which would satisfy an objective observer that the person concerned may have committed the offence and further must be judged against all the circumstances of the case. See also *Murray (Margaret)* v *UK* (1994), *O'Hara* v *UK* (2002)). This does not include preventative detention (see *Jecius* v *Lithuania* (2002)).

■ Detention of individuals who breach court orders (see *Benham* v *UK* (1996)).

■ Detention of minors, illegal immigrants and individuals with mental health problems (see *Ashingdane* v *UK* (1985) and *HL* v *UK* (2005)) or infectious diseases.

Further rights in Article 5

Article 5 also provides that arrested individuals must be informed promptly of the reason for their arrest and the charge against them, they must be brought promptly before a judge (or other person authorised by law to exercise judicial power, see *Brogan* v *UK* (1989)) and the individual should be tried within a reasonable time. Whether the respondent state exceeds the 'reasonable time' requirement by not releasing the suspect, the court will consider such factors as:

1 The complexity of the case, i.e. has the investigation taken an unusual amount of time due to the complicated issues involved, e.g. fraud cases. See *Muller* v *France* (1977).

2 The risk of collusion, i.e. is there a possibility of those involved conniving together to interfere with the investigation? Will the suspect improperly interfere with or put pressure upon witnesses? *Miszkurka* v *Poland* (2006).

3 The risk of the suspect fleeing the country; does the suspect have strong family connections, a home, business which prevent him from absconding?

4 The risk of the suspect reoffending. *Matznetter* v *Austria* (1969). Here, the court will take into account such factors as his previous record and character, and whether he is already on bail for another offence. *Letellier* v *France* (1991).

5 The risk that if released the suspect would be a danger to others.

When detained in a situation where they have not been arrested, an individual also has the right to a speedy decision by a court on the lawfulness of their detention (see *Winterwerp* v *The Netherlands* (1979), *SBC* v *UK* (2002)).

Clearly, Article 5 has a key application in relation to police powers, and this is explored further in later chapters on police powers and terrorism. However, the right applies to any detained individual, and has recently been found to apply where an individual is in 'informal' detention in a mental health hospital (see discussed below).

■ Article 6: the right to a fair trial

The right to a fair trial is provided for in Article 6, which has a number of key components:

■ it applies in both criminal and civil situations – specifically the determination of an individual's *civil rights or obligations*, or in any *criminal charge* against him; and

■ it states that he is entitled to a *fair and public hearing*;

■ which should be in *a reasonable time*;

■ by *an independent and impartial tribunal* established by law.

Determination of civil rights/obligations and criminal charges

The right to a fair trial relates either to an individual's civil rights and obligations, which has been given a wide interpretation, or to a criminal charge. In considering whether the charge is a criminal charge, the court will look at whether the state concerned classifies it as a criminal offence, and if they do not, then the court will examine the nature of the offence and the severity of the penalty incurred in making their decision (see *Engel* v *Netherlands* (1976)).

Fair and public hearing

The essence of any fair hearing is that there must exist 'equality of arms', i.e. that each party be allowed the reasonable opportunity to present their case without suffering a disadvantage (see *Rowe and Davis* v *UK*). In order for there to be a fair and public hearing there may be a need for the state to help the parties with legal advice and representation (see *Steel and Morris* discussed below). However, see the discussion of special advocates in the Terrorism chapter for an example of a court procedure in which there is clearly not equality of arms but the court procedure can be justified on national security grounds.

KEY CASE

Steel and Morris v *UK* (2005) *The Times*, 16 February (ECtHR)

Concerning: Article 6 and legal aid

Facts

In 1986, as part of a campaign against McDonald's in London, Helen Steel and David Morris produced a leaflet entitled 'What's wrong with McDonald's?' Headings in the leaflet included 'McDollars, McGreedy, McCancer, McMurder'… etc., and set out in writing allegations against McDonald's. McDonald's brought a libel action against them, and, due to a blanket ban on legal aid in libel hearings, they were forced to represent themselves, despite being on a very low wage. In the meantime, McDonald's employed senior Counsel with a great deal of experience in defamation law. Eventually, after 313 days (the longest trial in English legal history), they lost their case.

Legal principle

The court applied its own decision in *Airey* v *Ireland* (1979) and held that the complexity of the case and the difference in levels of legal support was so great as to give rise to unfairness, thereby breaching Article 6. It also held that the procedural unfairness and large award of damages was disproportionate and breached Art. 10.

Independent and impartial tribunal

The court has heard many cases on the definition of an independent and impartial tribunal. Both the appearance of impartiality and the reality are essential, and the court considers all the surrounding circumstances and features of the adjudication process in deciding whether the court or tribunal is truly independent and impartial. A good example of the court's methods can be found in two cases which the court decided on the same day in October 2003: *Cooper* v *UK*; *Grieves* v *UK* (2004). These are part of a series of cases brought by members of the armed services on the compliance of court martial proceedings with Article 6. In *Cooper*, the ECtHR found the RAF's court martial proceedings complied with Article 6, chiefly because of the role of the independent Judge Advocate and the Permanent President of Courts-Martial. In *Grieves*, the Navy's procedure was found to be in breach of Article 6 because it lacked these more independent elements.

In the recent case of *Othman (Abu Qatada)* v *UK* (2012), Article 6 has been used to prevent the deportation to Jordan of a terrorist suspect on the grounds that since the use of evidence obtained by torture is strictly prohibited, there would be a violation of Article 6 if the evidence of his two co-defendants, who had been subjected to torture, were permitted to be used against him at his retrial.

Further elements of Article 6

Article 6 goes on to provide that in any criminal trial, the accused shall be considered innocent until proven guilty, and sets out some minimum rights, including laws against self-incrimination. The applicant has the right not to be legally compelled into making statements or handing over documents which may be self-incriminating.

KEY CASE

Saunders v *UK* (1996) 23 EHRR 313

Concerning: self-incrimination

Facts

The Department of Trade and Industry were investigating the misconduct of a company (Guinness plc) which, they alleged, were falsely inflating the price of their shares as part of a successful takeover of another company (Distillers plc). During a number of interviews with the applicant (the chief executive of Guinness), he made certain involuntary statements which he was legally compelled to do; refusal would have constituted contempt of court under the Companies Act 1985. In the subsequent trial for various fraud offences, these statements were used by the prosecution as evidence of the applicant's guilt. The applicant complained to the Commission that being legally compelled to make statements which may incriminate himself if used at trial amounted to an unfair hearing under Article 6(1).

▶

Legal Principle

Once it was conceded that the statements were made under legal compulsion, the issue for the court was whether such statements could be used by the prosecution at the applicant's trial and, if so, whether this constituted an unfair hearing. The court said that the statements themselves did not have to be incriminating; it was enough if they were used in such a way as to question the innocence of the applicant. Since the involuntary statements made by the applicant at the interviews were a major part of the prosecution case, and were put before the jury as evidence of his guilt, that infringed the applicant's right not to incriminate himself. Therefore, there was a violation of Article 6(1).

📖 **REVISION NOTE**

Other areas of consideration within Article 6 include access to legal advice and the chance to cross-examine witnesses. See police powers II and contempt of court, respectively.

Under Article 6(1), a person must be brought before a tribunal within a reasonable time: for example, in *Neumeister* v *Austria (No. 1)* (1968), where seven years was not considered unreasonable due to enormous complexities of the case. But see *Blake* v *UK* (2007), where part of the proceedings lasted seven years. This was held to infringe Article 6(1) because the authorities failed to take the requisite steps to move the proceedings forward as required by the State's obligations. Also, in *Frydlender* v *France* (2000) a judgment after nearly six years was held to be manifestly excessive in the absence of the government giving any explanation for the delay.

■ Articles 8 to 11: permitted interference

Articles 8: the right to respect for private and family life, 9: the right to religious belief, 10: the right to freedom of expression, and 11: the right to freedom of association, are all similarly structured in that in paragraph one they contain a basic right, and in paragraph two they provide for that right to be removed in some circumstances. There are a number of hurdles that the state must overcome in order that the interference not be considered a violation of one of those Articles. Accordingly, before embarking on the separate interpretation of Articles 8, 9, 10 and 11 and their relevant case law, ask yourself all of the following questions.

1 Did the complaint fall within one of the rights protected by Articles 8–11? If yes, then

2 Was there an interference by the state with any of these rights? If yes, then

3 Was the interference of a type which was within the legitimate aims specifically stated in the relevant Article, e.g., national security, prevention of disorder or crime, etc.? If yes, then

4 Under the relevant Article, was this interference justified, e.g., in accordance with the law or prescribed by law? If yes, then

5 Were the measures taken by the public authorities 'necessary in a democratic society', the word 'necessary' meaning a 'pressing social need' which was proportionate to the legitimate aim pursued. If yes, then

The interference was justified and therefore was not a violation of the relevant Article.

Test	Definition
Prescribed by law	The interference with the right must be lawful under domestic law, and in line with EctHR standards. It must therefore:
	■ have a sound foundation in law, so the interference can be said to be regulated by law;
	■ the law must be sufficiently clear; and
	■ the law must be accessible to allow people to predict with reasonable certainty when and how their rights will be affected
Legitimate aim	The interference must be for one of the purposes outlined in the permitted restrictions. Therefore the state must be able to point to one of the reasons set out in Articles 8(2), 9(2), 10(2) or 11(2)) to justify the action they are taking. However, generally states are given leeway in regard to this leg.
Necessary in a democratic society (proportionality)	To comply with this leg, an interference must be
	■ a response to a pressing social need;
	■ a proportionate response to that pressing social need (proportionality is about balancing: could the aim have been achieved by less intrusive means?);
	■ and the reasons given by the state to justify the interference must be relevant and sufficient.

■ Article 8: the right to respect for private and family life

Article 8 protects the individual's right to private and family life, home and correspondence. This right can only be interfered with by a public authority where it is in the interests of national security, public safety or the economic well-being of the country, for the prevention of disorder or crime, for the protection of health or morals, or for the protection of the rights and freedoms of others. Also, as described above the interference must satisfy three conditions: it must be prescribed by law, it must have a legitimate aim, and it must be necessary in a democratic society.

Article 8 includes a positive obligation on the state to act in a manner which protects an individual's right to private and family life. It extends to the state being forced to recognise an individual's right to change their sex (see *Goodwin* v *UK* (2002)) and it forced the UK government to create a legislative structure to control when phone-tapping may be used (see *Malone* v *UK* (1984), *Halford* v *UK* (1997)). Furthermore, an individual's right to private life may extend to situations which might at first glance have appeared to be quite public situations. The question the court will ask is: has the person, in all the circumstances, a reasonable or legitimate expectation of privacy? (See chapter on privacy for more detailed discussion and key cases).

📖 **REVISION NOTE**

Cross-reference the discussion of Article 8 here with the Privacy chapter, which covers both ECtHR and domestic decisions.

■ Article 9: freedom of religion

Article 9(1) concerns not only the freedom to belong to a faith or possess different beliefs (which includes persons such as agnostics, atheists, pacifists, sceptics, etc.) but also to 'manifest' that religion or belief via the means of worship, teaching, practice and observance. Particular problems may arise where an individual wishes to manifest their belief by wearing some object or dressing in a manner which symbolises their adherence to a particular faith. Such demonstrations of one's religious affiliations may be legitimately restricted by the state to certain areas or institutions where there is a danger that civil strife may erupt if the freedom of religion was permitted to be practised in this way.

KEY CASE

Leyla Sahin v *Turkey* (2005) 44 EHRR 99
Concerning: manifesting one's own religion

Facts

The applicant, a student at the Istanbul University, complained that the university banning her from wearing the Islamic headscarf amounted to a breach of her right, *inter alia,* to manifest her religion, contrary to Article 9. Although the applicant accepted that

---

wearing an Islamic headscarf would not always be protected by freedom of religion, she argued, *inter alia,* that (1) university students were mature enough to be capable of deciding for themselves what was appropriate conduct; and (2) her choice had been based on religious conviction, which was the most important fundamental right that pluralistic, liberal democracy had granted her.

Legal principle

The Constitutional Court stated that granting legal recognition to a religious symbol of that type (i.e., Islamic headscarf) in institutions of higher education was not compatible with the principle that state education must be neutral, as it would be liable to generate conflicts between students with differing religious convictions or beliefs. The Grand Chamber confirmed the prior decision of the Chamber which acknowledged that the rules as laid down by the university were in keeping with the principles of preserving secularism and equality and were considered necessary in a democratic society. It was accepted by the court that (1) all students were free to manifest their religion 'within the limits imposed by educational organisational constraints'; (2) the restrictions were consistent with existing laws in operation and (3) it was recognised that the educational authorities were in a better position to know the requirements and needs of a specific course. Accordingly, the court found that the interference was justified and proportionate and therefore not in violation of Article 9.

Thus, it can be seen that not every act which is influenced by, or committed in the name of religion automatically comes within the protection of 'freedom of religion'.

Article 10: the right to freedom of expression

Paragraph 1 of Article 10 guarantees the right to freely hold opinions and to receive and impart information and ideas without interference by public authorities. The right does not prevent states from licensing broadcasters, cinema or television providers, however, and it is subject to exceptions. Paragraph 2 of Article 10 allows interference where that interference is in the interests of national security, territorial integrity or public safety; for the prevention of disorder or crime; for the protection of health or morals; for the protection of the reputation or rights of others; for preventing the disclosure of information received in confidence; or for maintaining the authority and impartiality of the judiciary.

Some key Article 10 principles include the following.

Principle	Case
There is a distinction between expression of opinion and expression of fact, and requiring individuals to prove the truth of their opinions in order to escape a criminal conviction is disproportionate.	*Lingens* v *Austria* (1986) 8 EHRR 407
Storing information on databases, and refusing access of citizens to that information, does not fall within the ambit of Article 10.	*Leander* v *Sweden* (1987) 9 EHRR 433
Punishing a journalist for publishing statements made by others in an interview would seriously impede the contribution of the press to discussions of matters of public interest. Punishment should only occur in these circumstances where there were very strong reasons for doing so.	*Jersild* v *Denmark* (1995) 19 EHRR 1
Portrayals of objects of religious veneration in a provocative way should be tolerated by members of that religion, but where the portrayal is a malicious violation of the spirit of tolerance, a key feature of a democratic society, it is permissible for a state to prevent that form of expression.	*Otto-Preminger Institute* v *Austria* (1995) 19 EHRR 34
Where the police exceed their powers or use their powers (in this case, breach of the peace) improperly to prevent peaceful demonstrations, their actions are not prescribed by law or proportionate.	*Steel and Others* v *UK* (1999) 28 EHRR 603
Imprisoning a lawyer for five days for being discourteous in court (where the discourteous comments were aimed at and limited to the manner in which the judges were trying the case) was disproportionately severe and could have a chilling effect on lawyers.	*Kyprianou* v *Cyprus* (2007) 44 EHRR 27

📖 **REVISION NOTE**

You should note that the list of permitted interferences with Article 10 is very similar to the list of permitted interferences with the right to private and family life in Article 8, with a few notable inclusions – the protection of reputation, the prevention of the disclosure of confidential information, and to maintain the authority and impartiality of the judiciary. For further discussions, see Privacy and Contempt of court chapters.

■ Article 11: freedom of assembly

ECHR Article 11: freedom of assembly and association

Everyone has the right to freedom of peaceful assembly and to freedom of association with others, including the right to form and join trade unions for the protection of his interests.

In line with Articles 8–10, the provisions in Paragraph 2 of Article 11 concern striking a fair balance between two competing deep-rooted rights: on the one hand, the right of individuals to assemble and demonstrate peacefully, and on the other hand, the rights of others to be protected from possible disturbances, violence and disorder resulting from permitting such a right. In this respect the state often faces a dilemma as to where the legal limits lie when considering the circumstances whether or not to intercede in permitting, or alternatively, prohibiting a particular demonstration from taking place.

Ollinger v *Austria* (2006) 46 EHRR 849

Concerning: when two opposing sides demonstrate

Facts

The applicant wished to hold a meeting (consisting of about seven people, in total) at a war memorial in a cemetery to commemorate the Jews who were killed there by the SS during the Second World War.

Another group, Comradeship IV (comprised mainly of former members of the SS) also wished to assemble there at the same time (as they had done for many years previously) for a ceremony in memory of the SS soldiers killed during the War. For fear of confrontation between the two groups, which might have led to public disorder and disturbance, the authorities prohibited the applicant from holding a meeting there. The applicant complained that his right to freedom of assembly had been violated.

Legal principle

The government argued that by permitting both sides to assemble and using preventive steps to keep the two groups from clashing, was 'not a viable alternative'. The court disagreed. (1) the applicant's assembly was to consist of only seven people; (2) the assembly itself was to be peaceful – no shouting or placards were to be used; and (3) ▶

even though in the past there were heated debates between the two groups, no actual violence had ever erupted. The court noted that, in the circumstances, the religious feelings of the cemetery visitors would not have been hurt had the applicant's group been allowed to assemble. Accordingly, the court found that the Constitutional Court gave insufficient consideration to the applicant's interest in holding the intended assembly and expressing his protest against the meeting of Comradeship IV, while giving too much weight to the interest of the others in being protected against some rather limited disturbances. Therefore, there was a violation of Article 11.

■ Article 14: the prohibition of discrimination

KEY STATUTE

ECHR Article 14: the prohibition of discrimination

Under Article 14, the rights in the Convention must be protected without discrimination on any ground, including sex, race, colour, language, religion, political or other opinion, national or social origin, association with a national minority, property, birth or other status.

The key to understanding Article 14 is to understand that it only protects individuals who have been discriminated against in the application of rights in the Convention. This means that an Article 14 claim can only be brought if it is 'piggy-backed' on to another Convention right. A good example of where Article 14 has been employed is by the House of Lords in the case of *A v Secretary of State for the Home Department* (2005), which is discussed in Chapter 6 on Terrorism.

📖 **REVISION NOTE**

Also see Discrimination chapter for a more detailed discussion of this particular Article.

■ Article 15: derogation from the ECHR

KEY STATUTE

ECHR Article 15: derogation

Article 15 states that where there is a war or other public emergency threatening the life of the nation, a state can suspend its obligations under the ECHR, to the extent strictly required by the exigencies of the situation, provided that the measures used are not inconsistent with other international law obligations.

This creates a two legged test: a state must be able to establish that:

1 There is a war or other public emergency which is threatening the life of the nation AND
2 The measures put in place which are affecting the rights of residents in the state are strictly required because of the emergency or war.

You should note that the rights to freedom from torture, inhumane and degrading treatment and the right to life, except where the death resulted from lawful acts of war, cannot ever be suspended in this way.

KEY CASE

Lawless v *Ireland* (1960) 1 EHRR 1

Concerning: Article 15

Facts

Lawless brought a case against Ireland after he was detained without trial for being a suspected IRA terrorist.

Legal principle

The court held that a public emergency is 'an exceptional situation of crisis or emergency that affects the whole population and constitutes a threat to the organised life of the community of which the state is composed'.

The UK government had a long-standing derogation in relation to extended pre-charge detention of IRA members. Similarly, the Turkish government has derogated from its Article 5 obligations to allow longer pre-charge detention in order to try to deal with Kurdish separatists, and in *Aksoy* v *Turkey* (1997) the court held that attacks by the PKK in South East Turkey constituted a public emergency justifying the derogation (but that 14 days pre-charge detention without judicial oversight could not be justified).

 Make your answer stand out

When answering an essay question on this topic, explain that the UK and Turkey have derogated from their responsibilities to deal with terrorism and consider detention periods for terrorist suspects under Article 5. This is discussed at more length in the Terrorism chapter, and a good discussion on when measures are strictly required by the exigencies of the situation is Lord Hoffmann's speech in *A* v *Secretary of State for the Home Department* (2005), and the Grand Chamber decision of *A and Others* v *UK* (2009).

■Putting it all together

Answer guidelines

See the essay question at the start of the chapter.

Approaching the question

This question is asking the student to discuss limits on rights, so a good answer would have to both *discuss* and *analyse* (using both case law and the text of the Convention) the points below.

Important points to include

- The margin of appreciation. Describe what the margin of appreciation is, when the margin of appreciation has been used, and critique the rule – is it appropriate in a globalised multicultural Europe?

- The ability of the state to interfere with certain rights in certain prescribed ways – you should discuss Articles 8 and 10, and explain when they can be interfered with. You need to describe and discuss the concepts of 'prescribed by law,' 'legitimate aim' and 'necessary in a democratic society (proportionality)'. Consider these concepts and the elements which make them up – an example is the decision by the House of Lords in *Gillan* (see Terrorism chapter) that the specific power to stop and search under ss 44 and 45 Terrorism Act 2000 was prescribed by law because the general policy had been published.

- The ability of the state to derogate from their obligations under the ECHR using Article 15. Discuss the requirements a state has to meet to derogate from its rights; explain that derogation is limited to certain rights and the fact that the power is subject to court oversight. However, consider whether courts really do interfere with the power of derogation.

 Make your answer stand out

It might seem tempting to stop there, but a good answer would go further. Detailed analysis of relevant cases will help on each 'bullet point': for example, when looking at whether courts do really interfere with the power of derogation, you could discuss, *Lawless* (1960), *Aksoy* v *Turkey* (1997), *A* v *Secretary of State for the Home Department* (2005).

Try to draw the threads of your answer together: clearly, states have the ability to interfere with human rights, but not all rights (for example, Article 3). Consider whether the powers the state has are too far-reaching or whether there are sufficient limits on the powers of the state to interfere with the rights of an individual.

READ TO IMPRESS

Baker, A. (2006) 'The enjoyment of rights and freedoms: a new conception of the "ambit" under Article 14', ECHR MLR, 69(5), 714–737.

Berry, E. (2006) The extra territorial reach of the ECHR, EPL, 12(4), 629–55

Palmer, S. (2006) A wrong turning: Article 3 ECHR and proportionality, CLJ, 65(2), 438–51.

Weekes R. (2005) 'Focus on ECHR, Article 2', JR, 10(1), 19–26.

www.pearsoned.co.uk/lawexpress

Go online to access more revision support including quizzes to test your knowledge, sample questions with answer guidelines, podcasts you can download, and more!

Police powers

3

Revision checklist

Essential points you should know:

- [ ] What constitutes a proper 'stop and search'
- [ ] Meaning of 'reasonable grounds' in relation to stop and search
- [ ] Knowledge of 'reasonable grounds' and 'test of necessity' for arrest
- [ ] Knowledge of the police powers to enter and search property
- [ ] The powers of the police to detain suspects after arrest
- [ ] The right of access to legal advice and how it can be delayed by the police
- [ ] Retention and destruction of DNA, fingerprints and other samples taken from suspects
- [ ] When evidence from an interview could be excluded because of oppression or unfairness
- [ ] The right to silence and when adverse inferences may be drawn

■ Topic map

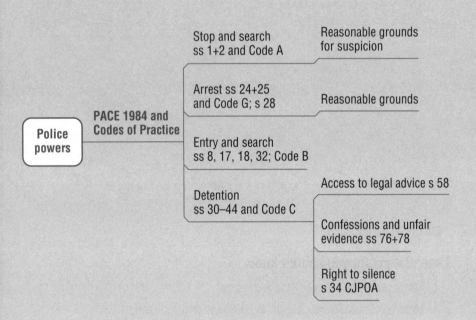

Stop and search
ss 1+2 and Code A

Reasonable grounds
for suspicion

Arrest ss 24+25
and Code G; s 28

Reasonable grounds

**PACE 1984 and
Codes of Practice**

**Police
powers**

Entry and search
ss 8, 17, 18, 32; Code B

Detention
ss 30–44 and Code C

Access to legal advice s 58

Confessions and unfair
evidence ss 76+78

Right to silence
s 34 CJPOA

A printable version of this topic map is available from **www.pearsoned.co.uk/lawexpress**

Introduction

The Police and Criminal Evidence Act 1984 ('PACE' or 'the Act') sets out the main framework regarding the numerous duties and powers of the police when stopping, searching, arresting, detaining, investigating and questioning suspects.

Included, as an integral part of the Act, are the Codes of Practice which set out the structure regulating police conduct towards suspects. The Codes of Practice are extremely helpful in interpreting various sections of the Act. It is important to understand that a failure to follow the relevant Code will not result in the action taken by the officer being immediately quashed, but may result in evidence being inadmissible at trial. The key ECHR right in this area is Article 5, because police powers are all about deprivation of liberty, but you should also bear in mind the rights which guarantee a fair trial in Article 6. Also see Articles 2 and 3 in relation to the treatment of suspects whilst in custody.

ASSESSMENT ADVICE

Essay questions

Essay questions on police powers are not too uncommon and generally centre round the difficulties of interpreting the Act, e.g. what constitutes 'reasonable grounds for suspicion' or the difficulties relating to those areas involving a lawful arrest. Questions also often centre around issues of the 'right of silence' and specifically the erosion of that right. In recent years the law has developed in this area and students should be advised to keep up to date with the latest conditions and case law. Students should be aware under what circumstances 'adverse inferences' may be drawn and especially how far you can rely on the legal advice of your solicitor to remain silent. It is also essential that you consider the many relevant cases. Again in-depth knowledge of the relevant Codes is invaluable. An essay question may also focus on a comparison between the Act itself and specific Articles of the ECHR.

Problem questions

Problem questions are by far the most popular type of question. Students generally have little difficulty in recognising the problem areas in the question. However, one major weakness is that they do not know how to properly apply the law they have stated to the specific issues in the question. The issues generally covered by the problem include such areas as an unreasonable stop and search; the suspect's right not to answer questions; unlawful arrest; no caution given; no reasons stated for the arrest; whether a confession

▶

ghest marks in this type of question come from spotting the more
...r example, what grade of police officer is authorised to delay access
... also from demonstrating wider understanding (for example pointing
... defence of entrapment in UK law, despite proposals in this area from
...sion in 1977).

Sample question

Could you answer this question? Below is a typical problem question that could arise on this topic. Guidelines on answering the question are included at the end of this chapter, whilst a sample essay question and guidance on tackling it can be found on the companion website.

PROBLEM QUESTION

James, who has four previous convictions for theft, is spotted by Police Constable Smith after coming out of a betting shop. The previous night a jewellery shop had been broken into and watches, gold rings and money were stolen. PC Smith notices that James is wearing a ring on his finger. He asks James from where he had purchased the ring, but no answer is given. PC Smith then proceeds to search James and discovers a Rolex watch and £500 in cash in a bag he is carrying. James says that he has just won the money by betting that Manchester United would beat Chelsea. 'A likely story', says PC Smith, 'You're coming with me'. 'On what charge?' asks James. PC Smith replies, 'I'll tell you later'. PC Smith then proceeds to take James to the nearest police station.

Advise James as to his legal rights.

Stop and search

The power of the police to stop and search members of the public is governed by sections 1 and 2 of PACE, and Code of Practice A (CoP A). You should also be aware that there are some restricted further circumstances in which the police may stop and search individuals. However, there is no general duty to answer police questions before arrest. This means that a failure to answer questions does not constitute obstruction of an officer in the execution of their duty: see *Rice* v *Connolly* (1966).

Under sections 1 and 2 and CoP A, a constable may search any person or vehicle and detain that person or the vehicle for the purpose of the search. The search can only be carried out to look for certain items, most importantly stolen items and prohibited items (i.e. offensive weapons and articles adapted for or used for criminal offences). Crucially, a constable may only stop and search an individual if they have **reasonable grounds for suspecting** that they will find one of these items.

KEY DEFINITION: Reasonable grounds for suspicion

It is essential that you understand that the term 'reasonable suspicion' is an objective test; reasonableness is not assessed simply by reference to the constable's opinion.

The reasonable grounds must exist before the person is stopped; a constable cannot stop in order to find grounds for a search (Para. 2.11, CoP A). Reasonable grounds for suspicion depend on the circumstances, but there must be an objective basis for the suspicion and it can never be based solely on generalisations stemming from personal factors without reliable supporting information (Para. 2.2, CoP A). It can, in unusual circumstances, exist on the basis of generalisations stemming from behaviour without supporting information, but it should normally be linked to some intelligence (Paras 2.3 and 2.4, CoP A). If reasonable grounds for suspicion cease to exist, the constable must not search that person, and, in the absence of any other power to detain, the person is free to leave (see *King* v *Gardiner* (1979)).

They cannot require the person being searched to remove any clothing in public other than an outer coat, jacket or gloves. Finally, if the constable is not in uniform, before commencing the search they must take reasonable steps to show that they are a police officer (see Sections 2 and 3 of PACE).

✎ EXAM TIP

PACE governs what the police can do, when they can do it, where they can do it, and how they must do it – you should make sure you are clear about each of these requirements. An easy way to pick up (or lose!) marks is to miss 'little' points in the question like whether the officer was in plain clothes. However, the key to an understanding of this particular area is to ensure you are very clear about the requirement for reasonable grounds for the officer's suspicion.

An excellent answer to a problem question could (and an essay question should) have reference to ECHR jurisprudence. The key cases here are *Engel* v *Netherlands* (1976) and *Guzzardi* v *Italy* (1980), in which the European Court held that Article 5 relates to deprivation of liberty, and will therefore not apply where there is simply restriction of movement. In deciding where to draw the line, regard should be had to criteria including the type, duration, effects and manner of the implementation of the measure. See especially the

▶

recent ECHR case of *Gillan and Quinton* v *UK* (2010) involving a police stop and search, where the court, on the facts, did not find it necessary to determine the issue of deprivation of liberty under Article 5, but instead did find a violation under Article 8, i.e. the right to respect for privacy.

KEY DEFINITIONS: Different types of offences

Offences are divided into three categories depending, in general terms, on their seriousness. **Summary offences** are the least serious offences and are dealt with by magistrates. **Indictable offences** are the most serious offences and are dealt with by the Crown Court. **Either-way offences** fall in between and can be tried in either category depending on how serious the offence was – there is a sliding scale which takes into account a range of factors. Some police powers can only be exercised where the offence is an indictable offence, and this will include offences which are triable either way. Knowledge of the differences between these offences is particularly relevant to arrest conditions (see below).

■ Arrest

PACE does not define arrest, but merely lays down conditions: the definition of arrest has been left to the courts. There is a great deal of case law on the subject, but in essence there are three elements:

1 a submission by the arrested party, or physical restraint enforcing the arrest;
2 the arrestor must signify by clear words that he is arresting the other party as soon as is practicable (see PACE ss 28(1) and (5), discussed below); and
3 the arrestor must make the grounds for the arrest clear as soon as is practicable (see PACE s 28(3)).

Arrest powers

The key power of arrest is arrest without a warrant by a police officer under section 24 of PACE (as amended by the Serious and Organised Crime and Police Act 2005 (SOCAP 2005) and CoP G. Prior to the amendments introduced by SOCAP, arrest was based on the concept of 'arrestable offences' and unless the **offence** fell into the categories of arrestable offences, the constable could not arrest. However, since 31 December 2005, the arrest powers for police officers have been fundamentally restructured.

Arrest can also be carried out where a magistrate has issued a warrant or where there is a breach of the peace. Furthermore, section 25 of PACE also gives a citizen's power of arrest where an indictable offence is being committed.

Breach of the peace

Every citizen, including police officers, has the power to arrest where there is a breach of the peace. Where the arrest is on the basis of an apprehended breach of the peace, the power to arrest should only be used exceptionally, where there is a sufficiently serious and imminent threat. The key is that the police must be able to point to an imminent breach of the peace, and, where they can, the response to that imminent breach must be proportionate (see the case in Public Order of *R (on the application of Laporte)* v *Chief Constable of Gloucestershire* (2006) – a case in which the police lost on both elements).

■ Arrest under PACE

The power of the police to arrest without a warrant is governed by section 24 of PACE and CoP G.

KEY STATUTE

Police and Criminal Evidence Act 1984, s 24

Section 24 gives a general power of arrest to a constable where an individual is committing or is about to commit an offence, or where the constable has reasonable grounds for suspecting the person is going to or is already committing an offence. If the constable has reasonable grounds for suspecting an offence has been committed, he can arrest anyone who he has reasonable grounds to suspect of being guilty.

However, this power is only exercisable where a constable has reasonable grounds for believing that the arrest is necessary because one of the reasons in s 24(5) is met.

The necessary reasons mentioned in s 24(4) are set out in s 24(5) and include:

■ giving the police time to check the name or address of the person arrested;

■ preventing the arrested person from causing or suffering physical injury or damage to property;

■ allowing effective investigation of an offence;

■ preventing the arrested person from disappearing.

Therefore, a lawful arrest requires a two-stage approach:

1 a constable knowing or having reasonable grounds for suspecting a person to be guilty of an offence; and

2 a constable having reasonable grounds for believing that person's arrest to be necessary. The reasonable grounds must be objective and be based on one, or more, of the reasons in section 24(5).

Reasonable grounds for suspecting a person is guilty

The leading case is *Castorina* v *Chief Constable of Surrey* (1988), in which the Court of Appeal laid down a three-condition test:

1 Did the constable suspect that the arrested person was guilty of the offence? (subjective element)
2 Did the constable have reasonable proof of that suspicion? (objective element)
3 If the answer to both is yes, then the constable met the test as long as the arrest was not *Wednesbury* unreasonable – it must have been made taking into account all relevant factors and ignoring all non-relevant issues; it must have been made for a proper purpose; and it must not be one which a reasonable officer could not have come to.

Reasonable grounds for believing the arrest to be necessary

The criteria are set out in s 24(5) and some further guidance is given in CoP G. This states that the constable has a discretion as to what action to take and which reason is to be applied (Para. 2.4, CoP G), but at least one reason must be satisfied (Para. 2.5, CoP G) and the criteria are exhaustive (Para. 2.7, CoP G).

KEY CASE

Richardson v *Chief Constable of West Midlands Police* (2011) EWHC 733 (QB)

Concerning: whether the arrest is necessary

Facts

An incident occurred at a school which gave rise to allegations against a teacher, the claimant, that he had assaulted a pupil. By agreement, on 16 December 2009 the claimant and his solicitor voluntarily attended the police station to answer questions about the alleged assault. Whilst there, the claimant was arrested. The allegations were subsequently dropped. In his claim for, *inter alia*, wrongful arrest against the police, the claimant submitted that there were no reasonable grounds for the arresting officer to believe that the arrest was necessary.

Legal principle

Applying the above *Castorina* test, the issue of a lawful arrest is a question of fact to be determined by the court. In this instance, the custody officer justified his arrest on the grounds that 'the practical and sensible option was arrest and detention'. Since, as a volunteer, the claimant would be free to leave before the interview was fully completed, this might lead to complications later on about his status and cause problems about being arrested, which in turn might prejudice the investigation. The court stated that since the claimant voluntarily attended the police station, and since there was no evidence to suggest that he was likely to leave before the end of his interview, the arrest itself was unlawful. As a result, his claim for false imprisonment succeeded.

In deciding the 'necessity for arrest' factor, the Code (Para. 2.6, CoP G), the constable must 'justify the reason or reasons why a person needs to be taken to a police station for a custody officer to decide whether the person should be placed in police detention, and the constable must take into account the situation of the victim, the nature of the offence, the circumstances of the suspect and the needs of the investigative process' (Para. 2.8, CoP G). For a recent Court of Appeal case, see *Hayes* v *Chief Constable of Merseyside* (2011), where the court affirmed the 'two-stage test', and especially that a police officer must consider, from an objective viewpoint, whether the arrest was necessary for any of the reasons stated in s 25(a)–(e).

✎ EXAM TIP

Remember, merely having the power to arrest does not automatically entitle the constable to arrest without further consideration. The responsibility in arrest situations lies solely with the arresting officer, not with his superiors, and hence it is his discretion and his judgement that is all-important. Accordingly, it is for the constable to examine and justify his reasons why, in the particular case, the arrest was necessary. Consider both elements of the 'arrest' test: the police must prove that they had reasonable grounds for suspecting the individual's involvement and they must have objective grounds for believing the arrest to be necessary. Missing out either leg, or failing to explain the 'three-condition test' in *Castorina* would result in a very poor answer. Also, when discussing 'reasonable grounds for arrest' issues do not lose sight of the relevant ECHR cases, particularly *Fox, Hartley and Campbell* v *UK*; *O'Hara* v *UK* (1991).

Informing the arrested party

Section 28 of PACE provides that arrest is not lawful unless the person arrested is informed that he is under arrest and the grounds for the arrest as soon as is practicable after the arrest (s 28(1) and (3)) The suspect must be told, at least, the relevant circumstances of the arrest, as known by the police officer. This is true whether or not the fact of the arrest or the grounds for it are obvious. There is no doubt that the degree of detail that must be told to the suspect to the relevant circumstances of the arrest will vary from case to case. For example, in *Murphy* v *Oxford* (1985) the suspect was informed that he was being arrested on suspicion of burglary in Newquay. The Court of Appeal held that, since no mention was made of the fact of the date or that it was a hotel in Newquay that was burgled, the arrest was unlawful.

■ Powers to enter and search

PACE has four sections that permit the police to enter and search premises in different circumstances. Under s 8 a magistrate may issue a warrant to enter and search premises for evidence of an indictable offence – see *R (Bhattiv)* v *Croydon Magistrates' Court* (2010). Section 17 deals with entry and search without a warrant – see *Friswell* v *Chief Constable of Essex* (2004). Section 18 concerns entry and search after arrest – see *Jeffrey* v *Black* (1978). Finally, section 32 deals with searches of a person away from a police station – see *Collman* v *DPP* (2003).

> ✎ **EXAM TIP**
>
> Like stop and search and arrest, it is crucial that you are aware of all the elements of each section which allow the police to enter and search property. Classic scenarios that catch students out include searches of a property under Section 8 where the arrest was under Section 24 or arresting an individual in the street and then going to search their property under Section 32.

■ Detention

PACE sets out the rules on detention of arrested individuals in sections 30–44. It requires regular reviews to be taken of the detention and, in sections 41–4, maximum time limits for the detention are set out.

> ✎ **EXAM TIP**
>
> You should be aware of the maximum periods allowed before the police are required to seek authorisation from the magistrates for further extensions – the maximum period of detention being 96 hours in total (excluding terrorist offences). As explained above, problem questions will typically include that of a suspect being held for too long or a junior officer authorising their detention. These are easy marks to pick up if you are clear about the rules.

■ Access to legal advice

The right of access to legal advice when arrested is fundamental. It is not explicitly set out in the ECHR but has been developed by the court through the combined application of Article 6(1) and 6(3)(c) (see, for example, *Murray* v *UK* (1994), in which a 48-hour delay in granting access to legal advice was held to be a breach of Article 6(1) and 6(3)(c). Also see *Averill* v *UK* (2001) where a denial of access for 24 hours constituted a breach).

In the UK, there is no right of legal advice at common law, and the right was first given statutory force in section 58 of PACE. Apart from section 58 of PACE it is essential that students are familiar with Code of Practice C and, in particular, Annex B.

PACE, s 58 – the right of access to legal advice

Section 58 guarantees a person who has been arrested and held in custody the right to consult a solicitor privately at any time, although this right can be delayed for up to a maximum of 36 hours in certain circumstances.

To prevent an arrested person from seeing a solicitor, the offence must be an indictable one; there must be authorisation from a superintendent or more senior officer (although this can be a more junior officer acting up in some circumstances: see *R* v *Alladice* (1988), discussed below); and the police must show that they have reasonable grounds for believing that (s 58(8)):

(a) exercise of the right will lead to interference with or harm to evidence connected with an indictable offence or interference with or physical injury to others, or

(b) it will lead to the alerting of others suspected but not yet arrested, or

(a) will hinder the recovery of any property obtained as a result of the offence, or

(b) the person detained has benefited from his criminal conduct and the recovery of the property constituting the benefit will be hindered by the right to see a solicitor.

The right to inform someone of your arrest is set out in section 56. Where the police wish to delay the arrested person from telling another individual about their arrest, they must be able to point to a specific reason, as with section 58. However, in this case the authorisation need only come from an inspector or more senior officer.

Since the introduction of the right to see a lawyer, a considerable amount of case law has built up. Some examples are given below; the key cases are those of *Samuel* and *Alladice*.

Case	Decision
R v *Samuel* (1988) 87 Cr App R 232	In this case, the superintendent had no grounds for deciding that the experienced and respected solicitor who was stopped from seeing his client would warn others or hinder the recovery of stolen property. The police have to believe that one of the occurrences in s 58(8) will occur, not just that it might. The refusal to allow Samuel to see a solicitor was therefore unjustified, and the impact of his lack of legal advice was that his conviction was quashed. It was held that the interview in which he confessed was unlawful and so the evidence from it should not be admitted because it was so unfair (see the discussion of s 78 of PACE below). ▶

Case	Decision
R v *Alladice* (1988) 87 Cr App R 380	Again the police breached s 58 by unjustifiably refusing access to a solicitor. However, in Alladice the court found that lack of access to a solicitor did not make his confession unreliable so that it could be struck out at trial and, furthermore, access to a solicitor would have added nothing to the defendant's understanding of his rights, therefore the conviction was upheld. Therefore breach of s 58 does not automatically mean that statements made by the defendant are inadmissible at their trial.
R v *James* [2004] EWCA Crim 1433	The conviction in 1986 of James was held to be unsafe because it was based on interviews by the police in which there had been breaches of PACE, including s 58, and he was therefore released in 2004. The arrest of the defendant had taken place only a few days after PACE came into force, and the police did not apply the strict test of s 58 as they should have done. They did not refuse access to the duty solicitor on the basis of s 58(8) but for other reasons, which therefore constituted a clear breach of s 58.
R (on the application of Malik) v *Chief Constable of Greater Manchester* [2006] EWHC 2396 (Admin)	Although this is a judicial review case relating to offences under the Terrorism Act 2000, to which s 58 does not apply, the court applied the principles of s 58. It found that it was reasonable to refuse access to a particular solicitor who the police suspected might have been a witness to or part of the conspiracy they were investigating. They had not refused access to a different solicitor – the duty solicitor was available to the defendant – so they had not acted unreasonably and the application for judicial review was refused.

! Don't be tempted to . . .

Narrow revision is very dangerous here, as it so often is. Students should also be familiar with the law relating to the right of access to legal advice *prior* to suspects being questioned at the police station. See especially the recent Supreme Court decisions of *Cadder* v *HM Advocate* (2010) and *Ambrose* v *Harris; HM Advocate* v *M; HM Advocate* v *G* (2011).

Questions on s 58 access will usually require you to consider the reasonableness of the justification by the police. When doing so, make sure first of all that the reasons for delay fall into the categories in s 58(8) and then consider the reasonableness of the delay. Reading and understanding *Samuel* and *Alladice* is essential. Questions like this will also need a detailed application of ss 76 and 78 (see below) to consider whether the evidence, if obtained through a breach of s 58, should be excluded by the court.

■ Retention/destruction of fingerprints and samples under sections 63 and 64 of PACE

The taking of both intimate and non-intimate samples from a suspect are governed by section 62 and section 63, and later amended by section 10 CJA 2003 (non-intimate samples), which take account of advances in DNA technology and its use in court as evidence, and also reclassified certain samples. Section 64 of PACE deals with the restriction on use and the destruction of fingerprints, impressions of footwear and samples. Prior to the amended section 64, it used to be the case that when a defendant had been acquitted of a crime, or discharged, all related fingerprints and samples taken from that person had to be destroyed. However, in *Attorney-General's Reference (No 3 of 1999)* (2001) the House of Lords said that, where a saliva sample had been unlawfully retained, that did not automatically mean that such evidence was excluded at trial: its admissibility was a matter of discretion for the particular judge. Accordingly, evidence so admitted did not amount to an unlawful interference by the state into the defendant's private life under Article 8.

At present, under s 64(1A) of PACE, exceptions excluded, the state is permitted to retain fingerprints and DNA samples indefinitely of innocent individuals for future police investigations into criminal offences which have not yet occurred. See, for example, the decision in the case of *R (S and Marper)* v *Chief Constable of South Yorkshire Police* (2004). However, in *S and Marper* v *UK* (2008), the European Court of Human Rights declared that such indefinite retention constituted a violation of Article 8.

KEY CASE

R (on the application of GC) v *Commissioner of Police of the Metropolis* [2011] UKSC 21

Concerning: destruction of DNA and fingerprint samples under s 64 of PACE

Facts

The Supreme Court heard an appeal by two suspects whose DNA and fingerprints were taken by the police. The first appellant, GC, was released without being charged; the ▶

second appellant, C, was charged but was subsequently acquitted. Their requests for their samples to be destroyed were refused.

Legal principle

The Supreme Court held that the present law regarding the indefinite retention of samples, save in exceptional circumstances, amounted to a violation of Article 8 of the ECHR. Accordingly, the appeal was allowed.

 Make your answer stand out

The law with regard to police powers is developing rapidly. You have to keep up with these changes. For example, you should take particular note that at the time of writing the Protection of Freedoms Bill is going through Parliament, which, if passed, will affect a number of existing statutory provisions, including PACE. Examples include expected new laws relating to the retention/destruction of fingerprints and DNA data under sections 63 and 64 of PACE. Further, the potential new legislation is expected to include such additions as a code of practice relating to the powers of entry on to premises, and stop and search provisions, as well as changes to the detention periods under the Terrorism Act 2000, and the reduction of detention for terrorist suspects from the present 28 days to 14 days. Students who cite the latest law and cases will impress the examiners and no doubt gain those extra vital marks.

■ Confessions and excluding unfair Evidence (s 76 and s 78 PACE)

At common law, the general rule is that evidence which has been improperly obtained will not automatically be excluded from the trial. The test is whether the evidence is relevant, and if it is, it is admissible. However, confessions do not fall under this rule because of their importance in a defendant's trial, and where they were obtained by 'unfair inducements' they were excluded. Since the introduction of PACE, confessions and other evidence can be excluded under two sections: s 76 and s 78.

Oppression and unreliability (s 76 PACE)

KEY STATUTE

PACE, s 76 – confessions

Section 76 provides that a confession may be given in evidence if it is relevant and not excluded.

The court must exclude the confession if the individual who confessed tells the court that the confession was obtained, or might have been obtained by:

(1)   Oppression, or

(2)   In consequence of anything said or done which might make it unreliable.

However, the confession can be reincluded as evidence if the prosecution proves beyond reasonable doubt that the confession was not obtained in this way.

Under s 76, a confession – defined in s 82 PACE as an adverse statement – must be excluded where it is obtained through oppression or where circumstances make the confession unreliable. As soon as the allegation of a breach of s 76 is raised, it is for the Crown (who has the legal burden) to prove that there was no breach – it is not the defendant's duty to prove that oppression or something else did take place.

Oppression

Oppression is far harder to establish than circumstances leading to unreliability. The courts have held that oppression is to be given its ordinary dictionary meaning, and that oppression will virtually always involve some impropriety on the part of the police. Leading cases include *R* v *Fulling* (1987), in which the action of the police in telling the defendant that her boyfriend had been having a long-standing affair, leading to her subsequent confession, was not held to be sufficiently harsh or wrongful to qualify. A key case is *R* v *Paris, Abdullahi, Miller.*

KEY CASE

R v *Paris, Abdullahi, Miller* (1993) 97 Ct App R 99

Concerning: oppression

Facts

The three men were convicted of the murder of a prostitute, with whom Miller was living before her murder. The chief evidence against them was a confession by Miller, which he gave after he had denied the charge over 300 times in the face of serious police intimidation.

Legal principle

Given the 'length and the tenor' of the police interviews they ought not to have been admitted as evidence, and although it is appropriate for the police to pursue a course of questioning and refuse to accept a denial by a defendant, it is undoubtedly oppressive to shout over 300 times that the defendant is guilty.

Unreliability

As stated above, something said or done, in the circumstances existing, which is likely to lead to unreliability is an easier matter to establish for defendants. The defendant needs to establish:

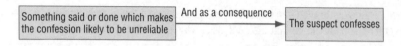

A good example of this is the case of *R* v *Samuel* (2005):

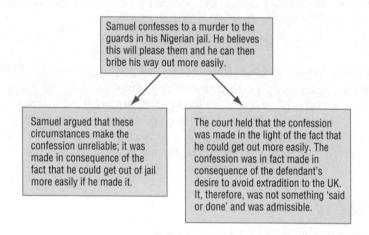

A leading case on unreliability is the case of *Chung*.

KEY CASE

R v *Howard Chung* (1991) 92 Crim App R 314

Concerning: something said or done which is likely to render the confession unreliable

Facts

After his arrest for a stolen vehicle, police refused to allow the defendant to see a solicitor, and instead took him back to his flat to search it. In the flat they found evidence of motor insurance fraud. The police officers then alleged that the defendant confessed to selling documents on but no note was made of his confession. When they returned to the police station, the police made a note and the four officers present at the search signed it but did not show it to the defendant. Furthermore, Chung was not allowed to see a solicitor until the following day, and upon being interviewed with his solicitor he was not shown the note.

Legal principle

The breaches of PACE – the refusal of his request to see a solicitor, the questioning without a solicitor present, the failure to record the confession immediately, the failure to allow the defendant to sign the record and the fact that he was not told of its existence – all combined to make the confession unreliable.

Unfairness

Section 78 of PACE has a wider application than s 76, as it applies to all evidence, not just confessions, and it gives the court a general discretion to exclude evidence, rather than obliging the court to exclude it as with s 76.

KEY STATUTE

PACE, s 78

Under s 78, the court, having regard to all the circumstances, can refuse to allow evidence if 'the admission of the evidence would have such an adverse effect of the fairness of the trial that the court ought not to admit it' (s 78(1)).

A breach of PACE may fall into this category, but will not always – it is for the court to decide if the breach has caused an unfairness which will have a sufficiently adverse effect on the fairness of the trial. For example, in *R* v *Ibrahim and Others* (2008), under s 34(2A) of the CJPOA 1994 where, before being questioned, the suspect had not been permitted to consult with a solicitor. In such circumstances, adverse inference may not be drawn from any fact that he later relies on at trial. However, anything that a suspect may have said during his questioning may still be admissible at his trial.

Section 78 is the closest English law gets to a rule against entrapment because the court has used its discretion under this section to exclude evidence obtained by trickery or entrapment, but it is not obliged to. See, for example, the case of *R* v *Smurthwaite* (1994) and the ECtHR decision in *Teixeira de Castro* v *Portugal* (1998).

Exam questions will often present you with a statement extracted at interview and ask you to consider what the defendant ought to do about it. This situation will call both s 76 and s 78 into play, and you need to be clear about how each applies and what the advantages of each will be. Section 76 is more closely circumscribed – the statement must be a confession and therefore adverse to the defendant, and there must be an element of oppression or other circumstances making it unreliable – but once raised, the burden is on the prosecution to disprove. Section 78 is an easier test to meet, but it gives a wide discretion to the court and the defendant has the burden of proof. The question will usually require you to explain this and then apply it to the question, reaching a conclusion about which section might apply and whether the evidence could be excluded from the eventual court hearing.

Right to silence

Although English law traditionally gives a right to silence in the face of police questions (see the wording of the caution – Code of Practice C, para 10.5 – and the introduction to this chapter), this general principle has been seriously eroded in recent years, and there are now a number of situations in which silence will constitute evidence against the accused. Most controversial and far-reaching are provisions in the 1994 Criminal Justice and Public Order Act (CJPOA), which allow for adverse inferences at trial.

Adverse Inferences

The key provision is s 34 of CJPOA (although sections 35–37 also deal with situations where a suspect does not reveal or explain something to the police). Before the introduction of this rule, there were a number of high-profile comments on the failure of the legal system to deal properly with individuals who did not disclose something during interview which later formed part of their defence (see, for example, *per curiam* comments in *R* v *Alladice*, discussed above).

Criminal Justice and Public Order Act 1994, s 34

Section 34 CJPOA provides that arrested individuals who, when questioned by the police fail to mention a fact they could reasonably have been expected to mention and on which they later rely upon in their defence, are liable to have an adverse inference drawn when they reach trial. At this stage, it should be noted that sections 34, 36 and 37 have been amended by the Youth Justice and Criminal Evidence Act 1999, and especially section 58 in relation to adverse inferences.

One of the key cases on the application of s 34 is *Argent*.

R v *Argent* (1997) 2 Cr App Rep 27

Concerning: s 34 Criminal Justice and Public Order Act 1994

Facts

Argent was charged with stabbing a man outside a nightclub and, on his lawyer's advice, he refused to answer police questions in interview. He was convicted of manslaughter and appealed on the grounds that the judge had misdirected the jury on s 34. His appeal was dismissed and the court took the opportunity to lay down essential conditions for the use of the adverse inference in s 34.

Legal principle

Six conditions are necessary to draw an adverse inference:

1. There must be proceedings against a person for an offence.
2. The alleged failure must occur before a defendant is charged.
3. The alleged failure must occur during questioning under caution by a constable.
4. The constable's questioning must be directed to trying to discover whether or by whom the alleged offence had been committed.
5. The alleged failure by the defendant must be to mention any fact relied on in his defence in those proceedings. That raises two questions of fact (i.e. questions for the jury): first, is there some fact which the defendant has relied on in his defence; and secondly, did the defendant fail to mention it to the constable when he was being questioned?
6. When questioned, the defendant failed to mention a fact which in the circumstances existing at the time the accused could reasonably have been expected to mention.

Suspects must have had the chance to consult a solicitor prior to being questioned, otherwise the adverse inference cannot be drawn. This was a later amendment to the CJPOA following the EctHR decision against the UK in *Murray* v *UK* (1994) (discussed above) and other decisions on access to legal advice. See for example, *Condron* v *UK* (2001).

However, an adverse inference is not sufficient to convict on its own, and judges in criminal trials have to be very careful to ensure that they do not guide the jury in deciding why the defendant failed to mention the specific fact relied upon. See especially, the Judicial Studies Board (Specimen Direction 44): Defendant's Right to Silence Where Judge Directs Jury that no Adverse Inference Should be Drawn.

You should bear in mind that courts have struggled with an appropriate test to determine when reliance on legal advice will stop s 34 being applied to a defendant. Some developing cases on this question include *R* v *Betts and Hall* (2001), *R* v *Howell* (2003), *R* v *Hoare and Pierce* (2004) and *R* v *Beckles* (2004).

Beckles is the latest important word on this issue to date, and the Lord Chief Justice summarised the correct question as being 'whether the defendant *genuinely* and *reasonably* relied on legal advice to remain silent.'

✎ EXAM TIP

Students often struggle with s 34 in problem questions, so remember that it is all about whether the court is allowed to use the silence in interview to assume some degree of involvement in the crime: 'an adverse inference'. The key to any scenario where the suspect has kept quiet at interview and then later produced an alibi is to go through the steps in *Argent*: think about whether the suspect had been cautioned, whether the constable is asking questions about the offence and who committed it, whether the new fact is relied upon in the defence and the defendant failed to mention it when they reasonably should have done. If they refused to explain the fact, explain *Beckles* and consider whether they relied on legal advice and whether their reliance on that advice was genuine and reasonable.

✓ Make your answer stand out

Show that you know the context of s 34. For an interesting discussion of the law before s 34 and recommendations on bringing in an adverse inference for individuals who refused to answer police questions, see the Royal Commission Report on Criminal Procedure of 1981. Also see the recommendations of the 1993 Royal Commission on Criminal Justice, which formed the basis of the 1994 statute. Both of these reports emphasised the importance of receiving legal advice prior to drawing any adverse inference, a recommendation which was not included in the original s 34, and was only inserted after the European Court of Human Rights found against the UK in *Murray*.

■ Putting it all together

Answer guidelines

See the problem question at the start of the chapter.

Approaching the question

This question requires a structured approach, with a plan and headings in your answer. The stop, search, arrest and caution elements require separate consideration.

Important points to include

Was it legal to stop James? This requires an explanation of ss 1 and 2 of PACE and Code A, and the application of the law to the scenario; in particular, was there reasonable grounds for suspicion?

■ Was it reasonable for James to refuse to answer questions? Apply *Rice* v *Connolly*.

■ Was the search a legal search? Again, explain and apply ss 1 and 2 of PACE and Code A, including the procedural requirements which an officer must follow in conducting a search.

■ Was the arrest lawful? This requires an explanation of the arrest provisions in s 24 PACE and Code G, with a discussion of the criteria in *Castorina*, and an application of the law to the scenario. Again, the question is: does the officer have reasonable grounds for suspecting James? Furthermore, is the arrest necessary?

■ Was James properly cautioned? This requires an explanation of s 28 and the right to be informed of arrest.

The conclusion should bring together the stop and search and the arrest, and should identify all of the failures by the police.

 Make your answer stand out

An excellent answer is one in which you demonstrate further understanding of the legal context. In this question, it might include reference to Strasbourg case law and discussion of Article 5 ECHR, or explanation of the changes in arrest powers and discussion of how this scenario might have been different pre-SOCAP.

READ TO IMPRESS

Austin, R.C. (2007) 'The new powers of arrest: plus ca change: more of the same or major change', *Criminal Law Review*, June, 459–71.

Berger, M. (2007) 'Self-incrimination and the European Court of Human Rights: procedural issues in the enforcement of the right to silence', EHRLR, 5, 514–33.

Cape, E. (2012) 'Case comment – arrest', *Criminal Law Review*, 1, 35–9.

Cape, E. (2007) 'Modernising police powers – again?' *Criminal Law Review*, December, 934–48.

Roberts, A.J. (2006) 'Evidence: confession – Police and Criminal Evidence Act 1984 ss 76, 82(1)', Crim LR, Feb, 147–8.

www.pearsoned.co.uk/lawexpress

Go online to access more revision support including quizzes to test your knowledge, sample questions with answer guidelines, podcasts you can download, and more!

Public order

4

Revision checklist

Essential points you should know:

- [ ] Powers to arrest for breach of the peace
- [ ] The range of criminal offences related to public order
- [ ] The range of powers the police have been given to regulate meetings and processions

■Topic map

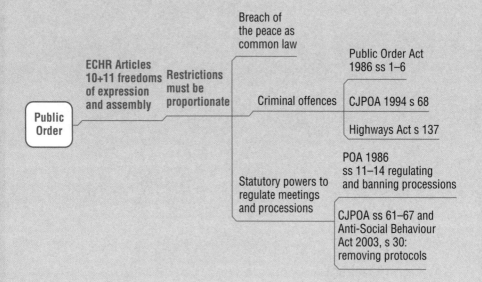

Public Order

ECHR Articles 10+11 freedoms of expression and assembly

Restrictions must be proportionate

Breach of the peace as common law

Criminal offences

Public Order Act 1986 ss 1–6

CJPOA 1994 s 68

Highways Act s 137

Statutory powers to regulate meetings and processions

POA 1986 ss 11–14 regulating and banning processions

CJPOA ss 61–67 and Anti-Social Behaviour Act 2003, s 30: removing protocols

A printable version of this topic map is available from **www.pearsoned.co.uk/lawexpress**

◼ Introduction

As with other civil liberties, the right to demonstrate is traditionally framed in a negative sense; individuals are free to protest so long as they do not commit violent or criminal acts.

Over time, the right to hold public meetings has gradually been constricted and placed under greater controls, so that holding a large meeting or procession in modern times requires police authorisation and will be subject to police conditions. However, since the introduction of the Human Rights Act 1998 the ability to assemble, express yourself and protest has become a positive right for all individuals.

ASSESSMENT ADVICE

Essay questions

There are lots of new developments in public order and the right to protest, with the European Court of Human Rights regularly hearing Article 10 and 11 cases and the government implementing new policies to deal with perceived criminal and antisocial behaviour. Essay questions might require you to analyse the overarching impact of the ECHR on public order law in England, or it might require you to discuss the development of a specific area of public order: for example, breach of the peace and public order offences.

Problem questions

Problem questions are common in this area. A typical problem question will describe a demonstration or public meeting which somehow gets out of control and ask you to analyse what offences might have been committed and what defences the individuals in the question might have. As with all problem questions, knowledge of the *actus reus* and *mens rea* of each offence is essential, as is knowledge of the potential defences. There will not be any 'dead weight' in the question, so read the question and analyse the scenario very carefully. It can often be worthwhile – where it is a long complex problem question – reading through the question and planning exactly how to deal with each aspect of the situation.

◼ Sample question

Could you answer this question? Below is a typical essay question that could arise on this topic. Guidelines on answering the question are included at the end of this chapter, whilst a sample problem question and guidance on tackling it can be found on the companion website.

The right to assemble

The freedom to assemble and protest is at the core of a free society. The key ECHR articles are 10 and 11 – freedom of expression and freedom of association (which explicitly includes the right to freedom of peaceful assembly). As well as the negative right to be allowed to demonstrate, these articles encompass the positive duty on the state to enable the protest to go ahead (e.g. by arresting violent counter-protesters).

The restrictions on assembly and protest can be divided into three main groups:

- breach of the peace (common law);
- criminal offences;
- statutory powers of the police to regulate meetings and processions.

Breach of the peace

□ REVISION NOTE

Breach of the peace is a very common tool used by the police to arrest would-be offenders. The leading case on breach of the peace is *R* v *Howell* (1981), in which Watkins LJ defined breach of the peace as a positive act which harms a person or their dwelling house, which is likely to cause such harm, or which puts someone in fear of such harm being done. This does not have to be unlawful, but must give rise to a real risk of violence.

Key breach of the peace cases for public order purposes are: *Duncan* v *Jones* (1936); *Piddington* v *Bates* (1961); *Moss* v *McLachlan* (1985); *Steel and Others* v *UK* (1999); *Redmond-Bate* v *DPP* (1999). A recent interesting and high-profile case on the use of breach of the peace in public protest situations is that of *Laporte*.

KEY CASE

R (on the application of Laporte) v *Chief Constable of Gloucestershire Constabulary* [2006] UKHL 55

Concerning: breach of the peace

Facts

Whilst on the way to an organised and legitimate demonstration outside a US airbase in Gloucestershire, the bus that the claimant was on was stopped and searched. A selection of items the police considered suspect was seized, including scarves, scissors, three crash helmets and five polycarbonate home-made shields. The police then concluded that the coach was going to the airbase, that some individuals on the coach were members of extremist protest movements and also that it was likely that allowing the coach to proceed would cause a breach of the peace. Therefore the police ordered that the coach return to London and escorted it back along the motorway. The claimant applied for judicial review in relation to both the decision to not allow the protestors to attend the demonstration and also the police action in forcibly sending the bus back to London.

Legal principle

The House of Lords held that no preventative action short of arrest could be taken where the perceived breach of the peace was not sufficiently imminent to justify arrest. In the present case, the police had acted unlawfully and disproportionately in restricting the claimant's Article 10 and 11 rights simply because they suspected that some of the individuals on the coach would cause disorder when the coach reached its destination where a large number of police officers would be in attendance.

✎ EXAM TIP

Breach of the peace is often regarded as a more flexible arrest power than the statutory powers of arrest in PACE, because it is based in common law. However, you should remember that there are vital elements which make up the power, and it crucial that an arresting officer can identify what a breach of the peace is and that it has occurred, or can establish that one is imminent. A problem question on breach of the peace is going to have something wrong with the way that the police exercised the power, and it is up to you to describe how breach of the peace should be used and what the officer did wrong.

However, apart from Articles 10 and 11 there is also the ever-present issue of a possible violation of Article 5 in relation to deprivation of liberty, e.g. police control over a large crowd of opposing supporters at a sporting event; or aiding the orderly exiting of people from an open air musical festival; or the cordoning off of an area after an accident.

Austin and Another v Commissioner of Police of the Metropolis **[2009] UKHL 5**

Concerning: breach of the peace and Article 5

Facts

Some 3000 demonstrators gathered in Oxford Circus. Thousands more gathered in the nearby streets. The organisers did not give notice of the event and refused to cooperate with the police. The appellants, who were involved in the demonstration, were prevented by a police cordon from leaving the area for some seven hours – known as 'kettling'. The police took this measure in order to prevent violence and the risk of injury to persons and damage to property. In due course the appellants brought actions against the police for false imprisonment and breach of Article 5. The lower courts and the Court of Appeal found no violation of Article 5. Thereafter they appealed to the House of Lords.

Legal principle

The House said that '[T]he ambit that is given to article 5 as to measures of crowd control must, of course, take account of the rights of the individual as well as the interests of the community. So any steps that are taken must be resorted to in *good faith* and must be *proportionate* to the situation which has made the measures *necessary*.' The Court found that the measures taken by the police under the circumstances were necessary to allow the protestors and others to eventually disperse safely. For those reasons the appeal was dismissed. See also the recent case of *R (on the application of Moos)* v *Commissioner of Police of the Metropolis* [2012] EWCA Civ 12, where the court also decided that 'kettling' was legitimate under extreme and exceptional circumstances.

A question on public protest and the use of breach of the peace is likely to require you to discuss the question of the imminence of the perceived breach of the peace. The key to imminence is the reasonableness of the belief of the police. If the police reasonably believe the breach of the peace is imminent, they can legitimately arrest. If the breach of the peace is not imminent, they cannot arrest or take any other action. Therefore, you will need to focus on the reasonableness of the police's belief that the breach is imminent in order to decide whether the arrest or other action is lawful.

◼ Criminal offences

You should know that the majority of the criminal offences used to prevent public disorder are contained in the Public Order Act 1986 (POA), especially sections 1–5. Also see ss 11–14 of the POA for the powers to regulate processions and meetings. Important consideration should also be given to key provisions in the CJPOA 1994 and the Highways Act 1980.

Remember that riot, violent disorder and affray all require the individual to intend violence or be aware that his conduct may be violent. Alternatively, for violent disorder and affray only, intending to threaten violence or being aware that his conduct will threaten violence will fulfil the *mens rea* element.

Riot

KEY STATUTE

Public Order Act 1986, s 1 – riot

A riot occurs when the conduct of at least 12 people – who are using or threatening unlawful violence for a common purpose – would cause someone of reasonable firmness to fear for their safety (although it is not necessary that someone of reasonable firmness be present). All those involved in using violence for the common purpose will be guilty of riot, and they do not have to use or threaten to use violence simultaneously. The common purpose can be inferred from conduct and the riot may occur in private as well as public places.

Violent disorder

KEY STATUTE

Public Order Act 1986, s 2 – violent disorder

Violent disorder occurs where at least 3 people use or threaten unlawful violence and, taken together, their conduct would cause a person of reasonable firmness to fear for their safety.

KEY CASE

R v *Mahroof* (1989) 88 Cr App R 317

Concerning: violent disorder

Facts

Four men, including the appellant and S, went to the home of the co-accused, B, to collect an overdue debt. Threats and violence occurred at B's home involving B, S and the appellant. The three were subsequently charged with violent disorder. The indictment only

▶

mentioned the three defendants, without including the other two men who were present. Both B and S were found not guilty of violent disorder. The appellant was convicted and appealed.

Legal principle

For violent disorder, there must be at least three persons present involved in the criminal activity associated with section 2, although, not necessarily those same persons stated in the indictment. Since two (B and S) out of the three accused had been acquitted the appellant must also be acquitted. If there was evidence of others involved, this should have been mentioned in the indictment. This was a material irregularity and the section 2 offence was therefore quashed, although in the appellant's case, a section 4 conviction was substituted.

Shouting 'kill the bill' and throwing bottles at the police has been held to constitute violent disorder, see *R* v *Hebron* (1989). Again, the violence need not be simultaneous, the person of reasonable firmness need not be there, and it may occur in private places. There is no need to show a 'common purpose'. See also the case of *R* v *W* (2010).

Affray

Public Order Act 1986, s 3 – affray

An individual is guilty of affray if they use or threaten unlawful violence towards another, and a third person of reasonable firmness would fear for their personal safety as a result. The threat cannot be manifested solely through words, and the person of reasonable firmness does not need to be present. The threat must be directed towards a specific person or people.

In *I* v *DPP* (2001), the House of Lords held that carrying petrol bombs in public did not constitute affray. It was held that carrying them was clearly threatening, but there was no one there who was threatened and a threat to the public at large is insufficient. The only people present were police officers and the group dispersed as soon as they met the officers.

Again, there is no need for a person of reasonable firmness to actually be present. In *R* v *Davison* (1992) Davison was arrested in his flat after threatening police officers who had been called to deal with a domestic violence incident with a knife, and the Court of Appeal held that the jury should only consider how a person of reasonable firmness would have reacted, not the police officers who were present.

Fear or provocation of violence

KEY STATUTE

Public Order Act 1986, s 4 – fear or provocation of violence

The offence of fear or provocation of violence (s 4 POA 1986) will be made out where an individual uses, distributes or displays threatening, abusive or insulting words or behaviour with the intention of causing another to believe that immediate unlawful violence will be used against him or another by any person. Alternatively the intention could be to provoke violence, or where it is likely that violence will be used or provoked. Insulting should be given its ordinary meaning and whilst interrupting play at Wimbledon affronted spectators, it would not necessarily insult them, as seen in the case of *Brutus* v *Cozens* (1972).

For s 4 offences, the speaker must take the audience as s/he finds them; it is not a defence to argue that the audience was particularly likely to be provoked, as in the case of *Jordan* v *Burgoyne* (1963) in which a National Front speaker in Trafalgar Square was found guilty of intending to provoke violence when he made anti-Semitic comments at a rally which included groups of Jewish people.

Harassment, alarm or distress

KEY STATUTE

Public Order Act 1986, ss 4A and 5 – harassment, alarm or distress

Section 4A is the offence of intentional harassment, alarm or distress, whilst s 5 is the general offence of harassment, alarm or distress.

Both are made out where someone causes harassment, alarm or distress because they use threatening, abusive or insulting words or behaviour, or disorderly behaviour, or they display any writing, sign or other visible representation which is threatening, abusive or insulting.

The person caused harassment, alarm or distress can include police officers but they must actually be harassed, alarmed or distressed; it is a subjective test.

For the more serious offence in s 4A, the individual must intend to cause harassment, alarm or distress. For s 5 to be made out, the individual must intend to behave in a disorderly way or be threatening abusive or insulting, but thereafter must simply cause the harassment, alarm or distress.

It is a defence to prove either that the conduct was reasonable or that the defendant was in a dwelling and 'had no reason to believe that the words or behaviour used, or the writing, sign or other visible representation displayed, would be heard or seen by a person outside that or any other dwelling'.

Dehal v *CPS* [2005] EWHC 2154 (Admin)

Concerning: intention under section 4A

Facts

The appellant entered a Sikh Temple and placed on the notice board a statement (in Punjabi) describing the President of the Temple, *inter alia*, as a liar, a hypocrite and a proud mad dog. As a result, the appellant was arrested and charged under section 4A.

Legal principle

On appeal, the High Court considered the relationship between section 4A and Article 10 of the Convention, and in particular whether under the circumstances (1) a prosecution was a proportional response to this conduct, and (2) whether Article 10 afforded him a defence. The court having examined the reasons for the decision declared that there was insufficient evidence to justify the initial bringing of a criminal prosecution in this instance. Such proceedings were considered to be a disproportionate response under Article 10(2), i.e. to prevent public disorder and/or for the protection of the rights of others, for the appellant's conduct. Accordingly, the appeal was allowed.

An offence under s 5 will only be made out if the offensive remarks or behaviour are seen or heard by others likely to be harassed, alarmed or distressed. See *Norwood* v *DPP* (2003): the prosecution has to prove two elements of the offence – (1) that the appellant intended, or was aware that the poster might be insulting and (2) the prosecution had to prove that the offensive remarks were within the hearing or sight of a person likely to be caused harassment, alarm or distress. See also, *Harvey* v *DPP* (2011).

Amongst the other defences that you should consider are whether the defendant had *reason to believe* that there was any person within hearing or sight who was *likely* to be caused harassment, alarm or distress, or that his conduct was reasonable.

Hammond (John) v *DPP* [2004] EWHC 69 (Admin)

Concerning: reasonableness, intention and s 5 POA 1986

Facts

The appellant (a preacher for some 20 years) displayed a sign to passers-by which read 'Stop Immorality; Stop Homosexuality; Stop Lesbianism'. Some people found the sign to be upsetting, distressing, insulting and annoying. He was arrested and eventually charged under section 5. It was found that even though the sign could not be considered threatening, or abusive, it was nevertheless insulting. Accordingly, the appellant's conduct could not be considered reasonable.

Legal principle

On appeal, the appellant argued, *inter alia*, whether the prosecution under section 5 was necessary or justified and a proportional response to his actions. The court, in agreement with the justices, found that although the sign itself was not expressed in intemperate language it was nevertheless insulting because the words related homosexuality and lesbianism to immorality. Accordingly the appeal was dismissed.

✎ EXAM TIP

A problem question on this area is likely to describe a scene where a group of individuals are in a public place and are behaving in some way which is unpleasant. In order to analyse where they are on the scale from riot to causing harassment, alarm or distress, you need to make sure you are clear on the distinctions between the different offences. This includes the mental element, the *mens rea*, and the available defences. The extra marks go to students who draw analogies with or distinguish from case law.

Aggravated trespass

Section 68 of the Criminal Justice and Public Order Act 1994 was introduced to deal mainly with hunt saboteurs but has a wider application (also see s 69).

KEY STATUTE

Criminal Justice and Public Order Act 1994, s 68 – aggravated trespass

Section 68 creates the offence of aggravated trespass, which is made out where an individual trespasses on land and does some act which is intended to either intimidate people carrying out lawful activity and to deter them from engaging in that activity, or to obstruct that activity, or to disrupt that activity.

Lawful activity is activity which the individuals may engage in on the land on that occasion without committing an offence or trespassing on the land.

KEY CASE

DPP v *Bayer and Others* [2004] 1 WLR 2856

Concerning: reasonableness under s 68

Facts

The defendants, having trespassed on to private land proceeded to attach themselves to tractors in order to disrupt the planting of genetically modified (GM) maize seeds by a farmer there. The sowing of these crops was being carried out on behalf of the government. The defendants were charged under section 68(1). They argued that their action was justified in preventing further damage to the environment and the adjoining land through pollution, and animal and soil transfer. At first instance the judge decided that, *inter alia,* 'taking into account those beliefs and fears, they acted with all the good intentions and that they had gone no further than was absolutely necessary to try and prevent the sowing of the crops'. Therefore, since their actions were reasonable in the circumstances, the charges were dismissed.

Legal principle

On appeal by the prosecutor, the court said that the first question should be: did the defendants use reasonable force in order to defend property from damage as a result of an unlawful or criminal act? In this instance the farmer was carrying out a lawful act and therefore the defence was not applicable in this case. If, on the other hand, the defendants honestly believed (subjective test) that the action was unlawful, the court should then ask whether they used no more force than was necessary (objective test) in the particular circumstances to alleviate the situation. Since the second question did not apply here, the appeal was allowed.

Wilful obstruction of the highway

KEY STATUTE

Highways Act 1980, s 137 – obstructing the highway

Section 137 states that a person, who without lawful authority or excuse, in any way wilfully obstructs the free passage along a highway is guilty of an offence and may be fined.

The leading case is that of *Hirst* v *Chief Constable of West Yorkshire.*

Hirst and Agu v *Chief Constable of West Yorkshire* (1987) 85 Cr App R 143

Concerning: wilfully obstructing the highway

Facts

A group of animal rights protestors who were protesting outside a furrier's shop were arrested for wilfully blocking the highway.

Legal principle

The Court of Appeal held that the correct approach to s 137 was:

(1)   whether there was an obstruction of the highway, which included any occupation, unless *de minimis*, of part of a road thus interfering with people having the use of the whole road;

(2)   whether the obstruction was wilful in the sense of deliberate; and

(3)   whether the obstruction was without lawful authority or excuse, which covered activities otherwise lawful in themselves which might or might not be reasonable depending on all the circumstances. In the present case, as the question whether the use of the highway was reasonable was not raised, the appeal was allowed and the convictions were quashed.

The key question therefore is: is the activity lawful and, if it is, is it reasonable so as to fall into the lawful excuse category? If it is not reasonable, it may not be covered by the lawful excuse category.

■ Serious Organised Crime and Police Act 2005 – 'The Parliament demonstrations'

Sections 132–138 of the Serious Organised Crime and Police Act 2005 (SOCPA) concern the limitations of demonstrating in the vicinity of Parliament and the powers of the police to control such demonstrations. Under section 132(1) where a demonstration occurs in a public place in a designated area, authorisation must be granted by the Commissioner of Police of the Metropolis before the protest may lawfully take place. Under s 134(4) the conditions attached to any authorisation may include imposing requirements on the place, the time, and the duration period of the demonstration. The most famous case to date to come to court (again and again) is that of Mr Brian Haw. Since June 2001 Mr Haw had been persistently demonstrating in Parliament Square against the war in Iraq.

R (Haw) v *Secretary of State for the Home Department and Another* [2006] EWCA Civ 532

Concerning: demonstration without authorisation

Facts

Mr Haw, having to acknowledge that he could not be discharged from the authorisation requirement under section 132, on 8 May 2006 sought authorisation to continue his demonstration. Authorisation was granted subject to a number of conditions under section 134(3). These included requirements that: (1) the demonstration area must not exceed three metres in width, depth and height; (2) Mr Haw was not to use articles in connection with the demonstration that would allow others to conceal items within them; and (3) he must maintain the site in a manner that allows any person present to tell that no suspicious items were present (such conditions were required in order to prevent possible terrorists from placing explosives and the like in that area). However, on 18 May 2006 proceedings were brought against Mr Haw for failing to comply with the above three conditions under section 134(3).

Legal principle

Before District Judge Purdy, it was argued that the measures imposed were ultra vires and/or incompatible with Articles 10 and 11 of the ECHR as they lacked precision and were impracticable for these purposes, and thus could not be described as being 'prescribed by law'. Whilst the judge accepted that the conditions were necessary for public safety reasons, under cross-examination of police witnesses it was found that the conditions lacked clarity and were unworkable. Accordingly, the conditions did not satisfy the requirements of reasonableness or certainty – being essential elements of the 'prescribed by law' principle under the Convention. On appeal by the prosecutor (*DPP* v *Haw* [2008] 1 WLR 379), the court refused to depart from the findings of the district judge and found that the specific conditions imposed were indeed unreasonable for lack of clarity and were unworkable. Accordingly, on that particular issue, the appeal was dismissed.

There are few modern-day individuals who represent the right to publicly protest more than Brian Haw, who has been protesting continuously in Parliament Square since 2001 on issues of global injustice. As well as the cases highlighted above, numerous legal challenges have been brought by the government to try to remove Mr Haw's ongoing protest, and sections of the Serious and Organised Crime and Police Act 2005 were intended to curtail his activities.

Hall, Haw and Others v *Mayor of London* [2010] EWCA Civ 817

Concerning: freedom of expression and demonstrations

Facts

In 2010 the 'Democracy Village' ('DV') in Parliament Square Gardens ('PSG') appeared to have suffered a serious setback via a decision of the Court of Appeal in Parliament Square Gardens ('PSG') which is managed by the Mayor of London on behalf of the Greater London Authority (GLA). The Mayor sought a possession order against those demonstrators. The demonstrators argued, *inter alia*, that their eviction would violate Article 10 of the European Convention on Human Rights.

Legal principle

One of the main issues to be resolved was whether, in the circumstances, such an order was proportionate. As a result of the continuing presence of the DV, the Court of Appeal found that: (1) the ability of others to demonstrate was curtailed; (2) people, such as visitors and the like, could be encumbered from wandering around that particular area; (3) the indefinite length of time that the DV remained there was unreasonable, and (4) overall concern about health and safety issues and the amount of damage that may be caused to that specific area. Under these circumstances, the court found that the interference was proportionate and that the Mayor was entitled to gain full control of the PSG.

Powers to regulate processions and meetings

Processions

Again, the key Act is the POA 1986. Sections 11 to 13 set out the powers of the police to regulate and ban public processions. The Act states that it only covers processions in a public place – defined in s 16 as a highway or a place to which at the material time the public or a section of the public has access, by payment or otherwise, as of right or by express or implied permission. The only definition of 'procession' comes from case law and it is 'not a mere body of persons: it is a body of persons moving along a route' (from *Flockhart* v *Robinson* (1950)).

Public Order Act 1986, s 11

Section 11 states that anyone planning a procession which is intended, amongst other purposes to demonstrate support for or opposition to the views or actions of any person or body of persons, has to give notice to the police, unless it is not reasonably practicable to give any advance notice.

For a procession to be customary, there must be sufficient consistency in the route, identity and nature of the procession for the police to be able to predict it and anticipate what regulation might be needed in relation to it (however, see *Kay* v *Commissioner of Police of the Metropolis* (2008) which related to organised mass cycle rides in London).

KEY STATUTE

Public Order Act 1986, s 12

Section 12 gives the senior police officer (i.e. the senior officer at the scene or, where the procession is pre-planned, the chief of police) the power to give directions imposing whatever conditions appear necessary to him to prevent disorder, damage, disruption or intimidation. This is only where the senior officer reasonably believes that the procession may result in serious public disorder, serious damage to property or serious disruption to the life of the community, or the organisers are arranging the protest to intimidate.

In the more extreme situations, where the chief officer of police reasonably believes that because of particular circumstances in a district or districts, the power to issue conditions under s 12 will not be sufficient to prevent serious public disorder arising from the procession, he can apply to the local council to have all marches banned under section 13 for a maximum period of three months.

✎ EXAM TIP

Problem questions on processions usually involve a scenario in which one or more marches have got out of hand. Students often spot the rioters and the other public order offences, but miss out on easy marks gained by commenting on whether the march had been in line with ss 11 and 12 and the procedural requirements of these sections. Bringing in discussion of the proportionality of any police actions and the requirements of Articles 10 and 11 will gain you the highest marks – look back at the ECHR chapter and consider how these controls relate to the rights to freedom of expression and association.

Assemblies

KEY STATUTE

Public Order Act 1986, s 14

Section 14 states that a senior police officer can impose conditions on an assembly where they reasonably believe that the result of the assembly will be serious public disorder, serious damage to property, serious disruption to the life of the community or that the purpose is intimidation. The conditions can include the maximum duration of

---

the meeting, the maximum number of attendees and the place which it will be held and they are such as appear necessary to him.

A public assembly is defined as an assembly of two or more persons in a public place which is wholly or partly open to the air (s 16 POA 1986). This was reduced from 20 people to 2 people by the Anti-social Behaviour Act 2003. Organising and attending an assembly and knowingly failing to comply with a condition is an offence, but it is a defence to prove this was because of circumstances beyond your control. Organisers can receive a three month jail sentence, and attendees may be fined.

The conditions imposed must be the minimum possible and they must be proportionate. An example of this can be found in *R (Brehony)* v *Chief Constable of Greater Manchester* (2005) in which the decision by a senior police officer to impose conditions banning an assembly for a set number of weeks was proportionate. It only restricted the group from demonstrating on one day a week over the Christmas period, an alternative site had been suggested, and the restriction was legitimately aimed at avoiding serious disruption in the town centre.

Trespassory assemblies

A prohibition on trespassory assemblies and offences relating to them was inserted by the CJPOA 1994 as s 14 A–4C POA 1986.

KEY STATUTE

Public Order Act 1986, ss 14A–14C

A chief of police can apply to the local council to ban all trespassory assemblies where he reasonably believes that an assembly is intended to be held on land to which the public has no right of access without permission (or where it will exceed any permission granted) and may result in either

(i) serious disruption to the life of the community, or

(ii) where the land, or a building or monument on it, is of historical, architectural, archaeological or scientific importance, in significant damage to the land, building or monument.

You should be aware that the meaning of trespassory has caused difficulties – s 14A(5) states that assemblies must be trespassory in the sense that the individuals are either on land they have no right to enter or are exceeding a limited right of access to land. The term 'limited' is defined in s 14A(9) to mean the use of the land is restricted to use for a particular purpose.

You should know the offences of organising or taking part in such a trespassory assembly.

Further police powers

The police also have powers to remove trespassers on land and to disperse groups. These powers are contained in section 61 of the Criminal Justice and Public Order Act 1994 and section 30 of the Anti-Social Behaviour Act 2003. Sections 63 – 67 CJPOA 1994 are also relevant and deal with 'raves'.

KEY STATUTE

Anti-Social Behaviour Act 2003, s 30

A senior officer may authorise his officers to exercise powers to direct individuals to disperse, and to direct non-residents to leave an area and not to come back for 24 hours. This can only occur where the senior officer believes that individuals have been intimidated, harassed, alarmed or distressed as a result of the presence or behaviour of groups of two or more persons in public places in any locality in his police area, and that antisocial behaviour is a significant and persistent problem in the area.

A high-profile situation in which s 30 was used was in Birmingham in 2005 when the police ordered the dispersal of a group who had gathered to protest at the staging of a play containing scenes critical of Sikhism. See *R (Singh and Others)* v *Chief Constable of West Midlands Police* (2005) in which the High Court held that s 30 applies to protests, and that the police acted proportionately in issuing and enforcing a dispersal of a demonstration inside and outside of the theatre.

✎ EXAM TIP

As with processions, the best marks are gained by applying the scenario or considering the essay question in the light of Articles 10 and 11 ECHR: freedom of expression and freedom of association. You need to know when these rights apply, and how they can be interfered with by the state. The key in problems scenarios is often likely to be the proportionality of the action by the police.

■ Putting it all together

Answer guidelines

See the essay question at the start of the chapter.

Approaching the question

This question requires an in-depth knowledge of certain sections of the POA 1986 and the common law. The key to answering questions of this type is to pick out the important words in the statement.

Important points to include

The question deals with issues such as 'the right to demonstrate', 'adequately protect' and, in particular, 'past judicial decisions'. Hence, knowledge of the different public order related case law is indispensable, e.g. *Piddington* v *Bates* (1961); *Beatty* v *Gillbanks* (1882); *Moss* v *McLachlan* (1985); *Thomas* v *Sawkins* (1935); *R (Laporte)* v *Chief Constable of Gloucestershire Constabulary* (2006); *DPP* v *Haw* (2007); these are but a small sample of the types of cases required which raise separate issues.

 Make your answer stand out

The question asks you to 'critically discuss'. Many students would, unfortunately, cite a few cases, accompanied by a few comments and think that the question has been answered. This alone would not be enough to get even half-decent marks. You must 'demonstrate' an ability to understand and discuss the main issues. Discuss whether the police have too much power when it comes to limiting the areas where demonstrations are legally permitted, or of banning demonstrations altogether. Identify the existing problems relating to static and movable demonstrations. Compare post- and anti-HRA, and specifically the difference, if any, of the effects Articles 10 and 11 have had on the interpretation of domestic legislation and the common law. Never omit a proper (not just two or three lines) and effective conclusion.

READ TO IMPRESS

Loveland, I. (2007) 'Public protest, public order and the Human Rights Act', *Legal Action,* October: 15.

Loveland, I. (2007) Public protest in Parliament Square, EHRLR, 3, 252–65.

Robins, J. (2007) 'Protesting too much?' *Law Society Gazette* 104(03), 22–3.

www.pearsoned.co.uk/lawexpress

Go online to access more revision support including quizzes to test your knowledge, sample questions with answer guidelines, podcasts you can download, and more!

Contempt of court

5

Revision checklist

Essential points you should know:

☐ The elements of contempt of court in section 2 of the Contempt of Court Act 1981

☐ The defences under CCA 1981

☐ When and how common law contempt of court can still be used to restrict freedom of expression

☐ Section 8 of the CCA and the secrecy of jury deliberations

☐ Section 10 of the CCA and the case law on the protection of sources for journalists

☐ The Coroners and Justice Act 2009 regarding anonymity of witnesses and fair trials

■Topic map

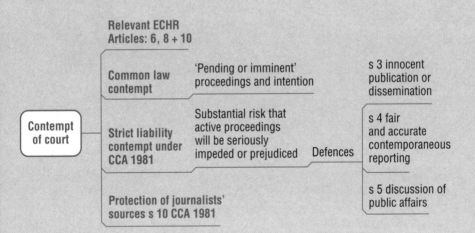

Relevant ECHR
Articles: 6, 8 + 10

Contempt
of court

Common law
contempt

'Pending or imminent'
proceedings and intention

Strict liability
contempt under
CCA 1981

Substantial risk that
active proceedings
will be seriously
impeded or prejudiced

Protection of journalists'
sources s 10 CCA 1981

Defences

s 3 innocent
publication or
dissemination

s 4 fair
and accurate
contemporaneous
reporting

s 5 discussion of
public affairs

A printable version of this topic map is available from **www.pearsoned.co.uk/lawexpress**

■ Introduction

The foundation of contempt of court is the right to a fair trial, and the consequent requirement of avoiding prejudice to a party to legal proceedings.

The conflict with freedom of expression arises most regularly in media reporting of high-profile cases, and the vast majority of the case law relates to actions against newspapers and other media. Contempt of court can be either criminal (i.e. interfering with the administration of justice, which can be in either criminal or civil cases) or civil (i.e. breaching a court order).

ASSESSMENT ADVICE

The general focus of questions on contempt of court and freedom of expression is on restrictions on the media and the tension between freedom of expression and the rights protected by contempt of court; the importance of the court process and the right to a fair trial.

Any question in this area will require you to apply and critique a provision of the Contempt of Court Act 1981 and case law which has interpreted the Act. Many will also expect you to understand the continuing relevance of the common law offences. As always, back up every point you make with authority and make sure you identify every element of the question – remember that no part of the question will be irrelevant.

Essay questions

Essay questions on contempt of court are sometimes set and may ask you to evaluate the extent to which the CCA 1981 achieves a fair balance between freedom of expression under Art. 10(1) and the exceptions in Art. 10(2), or to assess whether the defences under the CCA 1981 are sufficient to protect media freedom of expression and the public right to know. You do need to check your syllabus: did you study contempt of court as an aspect of freedom of expression? If so, then it will be relevant to any wider essay question on that right.

Problem questions

Problem questions are relatively common on contempt of court; it is a field in which the application of the statutory rules and key cases can be tested very well by fictional scenarios. You may be asked to advise a journalist intending to make a publication as to whether he faces any potential liability for that publication. It is important to check

▶

whether the requirements of both the statutory and the common law offences of contempt are met, since on some sets of facts there will be liability for one form of contempt but not the other. Small differences in facts can make a big difference: e.g. how long is it until trial of the relevant case? Are proceedings active? Will the case be heard by a jury or a judge? Don't forget that examiners are likely to want to test your understanding of the relevant defences.

■ Sample question

Could you answer this question? Below is a typical essay question that could arise on this topic. Guidelines on answering the question are included at the end of this chapter, whilst a sample problem question and guidance on tackling it can be found on the companion website.

ESSAY QUESTION

The Contempt of Court Act 1981 and contempt at common law unfairly restrain freedom of expression. Discuss, with reference to the Act and case law.

■ Background to the Contempt of Court Act 1981

The extremely important decision of *Sunday Times* v *UK* (1979) led to the Contempt of Court Act 1981 (CCA). The chief criticism in the ECtHR's decision was the failure of the House of Lords to balance the public interest in publication of the article against the pressing social need of protecting the authority of the judiciary. The EctHR concluded that the restraint was not proportionate. Prior to this Act, contempt of court had been based in common law. Following the CCA, common law contempt remains but has been limited to intentional contempt of court, whilst contempt of court regardless of intention is governed by the CCA. The CCA also clarified when contempt can be committed, reduced the scope of contempt and introduced new defences, most importantly, that of public interest.

■ Strict liability

One of the crucial features of the CCA 1981 is that there is no need to find an intention to commit the offence. In *Attorney-General* v *English* (1982), Lord Diplock stated that the public policy underlying this rule is deterrence.

KEY STATUTE

Contempt of Court Act 1981, ss 1 and 2

Section 1 involves the strict liability rule, i.e. intention is not required.

Under s 2(1) the strict liability rule is limited to publications, i.e. 'publication' includes any speech, writing, programme included in a cable programme service or other communication in whatever form, which is addressed to the public at large or any section of the public.

Also, under 2(2) it applies only to a publication which creates *a substantial risk* that the course of justice in the proceedings in question will be *seriously impeded or prejudiced*. 2(3) The strict liability rule applies to a publication only *if the proceedings in question are active*.

In order to fully comprehend the CCA it is essential that you understand the meanings and the courts' interpretation of the phrase 'substantial risk that the proceedings will be seriously impeded or prejudiced.' See, for example, the cases of *Attorney-General* v *English* (1982); *Attorney-General* v *News Group Newspapers* (1986); *Attorney-General* v *ITN* (1995); *Attorney-General* v *BBC* (1996); *Attorney-General* v *BBC* (2007) and the recent case of *Attorney-General* v *Associated Newspapers Ltd and Another* (2011).

The main principles in the CCA and the case law were distilled in 1997 in the case of *Attorney-General* v *Mirror Group Newspapers* (1997).

KEY CASE

Attorney-General v *Mirror Group Newspapers Ltd* [1997] 1 All ER 456

Concerning: strict liability in the CCA 1981

Facts

The case related to Geoffrey Knights, partner of Gillian Taylforth, arrested for assaulting another individual. Various newspapers carried high-profile articles about the trial, and the Attorney-General then brought contempt proceedings.

Legal principle

Schiemann set out the key principles which govern the application of the strict liability rule:

(1)   Each case must be decided on its own facts.

(2)   The court will look at each publication separately and test matters as at the time of publication. Earlier publications do not protect later publications, however.

▶

(3)   The publication must create some risk that the course of justice in the proceedings in question will be impeded or prejudiced by that publication.

(4)   That risk must be substantial.

(5)   The substantial risk must be that the course of justice in the proceedings in question will not only be impeded or prejudiced but seriously so.

(6)   The court will not convict of contempt unless it is sure that the publication has created this substantial risk of that serious effect on the course of justice.

(7)   In making an assessment the court will consider: (a) the likelihood of the publication coming to the attention of a potential juror (taking into account geographical circulation and numbers of issues published); (b) the likely impact of the publication on an ordinary reader at the time of publication (looking at the article's prominence and novelty); and (c) the residual impact of the publication on a notional juror at the time of trial. This last is the most important and the court will consider the length of time between publication and the likely date of the trial, the focusing effect of listening over a prolonged period to evidence in a case, and the likely effect of the judge's directions to a jury.

KEY CASE

Attorney-General v *Mirror Group Newspapers Ltd and News Group International Ltd* [2012] 1 Cr App R 1

Concerning: publishing stories about an arrestee, who was never charged with any offence

Facts

Soon after the murder of a young woman named Joanna Yeates, her landlord was arrested, but later released without charge. In the intervening period, the *Daily Mirror* wrote a front page headline 'Jo suspect is a peeping Tom', and included statements such as 'Arrest landlord spied on flat couple' and 'Friend in jail for paedophile crimes', and 'Cops now probe 36 year old murder'. *The Sun* also published various stories about the landlord, including the headline 'Murdered Jo: suspect "followed me" says woman', as well as other articles from people who had supposedly known the landlord. Thereafter, the Attorney-General issues proceeding against the respective publishers for contempt of court.

Legal principle

The court stated that the course of justice should not be interfered with. A publication that influences or is likely to deflect the proceedings from their normal direction would constitute an impediment, thus obviating the right to a fair trial. They declared that the vilification of a suspect constitutes one such risk to the course of justice. The court stated that the statements made by the *Daily Mirror's* publications asserting that the landlord's standard of behaviour, in sexual matters, were unacceptable. The articles in *The Sun* suggested that he was a stalker, had an obsession with death, had an unhealthy interest in blonde women, and had let himself into other occupants' flats. Such accusatorial statements led the court to conclude that, if the suspect had been charged with the murder offence, his defence would have been so undermined that the publications would have created a definite risk to a fair trial. Accordingly, a contempt of court was found to have been committed under s 1 and s 2(2).

Defences

Sections 3, 4 and 5 contain defences to the offence in section 2.

Innocent publication or distribution (s 3 CCA 1981)

As a publisher, it is a defence to show that you did not know and had no reason to suspect that proceedings were active. As a distributor, it is a defence to show that you did not know and had no reason to suspect that the material you were distributing was in contempt of court.

Contemporary reports of proceedings (s 4 CCA 1981)

Fair and accurate contemporary reporting of proceedings will not give rise to an offence. However, where the court considers it necessary to avoid prejudice, reports can be postponed for as long as is necessary under s 4(2). This power is only to be used as a last resort, and conditions have been set out for its use in case law. The key case is *MGN Pension Trustees* v *Bank of America National Trust* (1995) but also see the case of *Re B* (2006).

✎ EXAM TIP

Section 4(2) allows for fair and accurate discussion of ongoing cases, and thereby strikes a balance between the need to protect the defendant and the right to freedom of expression. In considering s 4(2), a good answer will emphasise this balancing act, and will note that s 4(2) orders are very restricted in their application – a judge wishing to make an order has to be very sure it is necessary, and, must also be aiming to postpone fair and accurate comment, not looking to avoid unfair comments arising out of the fair and accurate comment. The result of *Re B* is that much more emphasis is placed on editors and journalists to be responsible.

Discussion of public affairs (s 5 CCA 1981)

KEY STATUTE

Contempt of Court Act 1981, s 5

A publication made as or as part of a discussion *in good faith* of *public affairs or other matters of general public interest* is not to be treated as a contempt of court under the strict liability rule if the risk of impediment or prejudice to particular legal proceedings is *merely incidental to the discussion.*

Once the defence of discussion of public affairs has been raised, the burden of proof is on the prosecution. The normal meaning of 'good faith' refers to something done or said or written with honesty, sincerity and without malice. The key issue in s 5 cases is generally whether the risk of impediment or prejudice is merely incidental to the discussion.

The leading case on s 5 is the case of *Attorney-General* v *English* (1982). The House of Lords found that the article supporting the pro-life candidate did breach s 2 CCA 1981, but that the defence in s 5 was made out. Their Lordships held that if the article had failed to mention the candidate's pro-life stance it would 'depict her tilting at imaginary windmills'. The test of whether something is incidental to the discussion is not whether it could have been written as effectively without certain passages, but whether the passages are 'no more than an incidental consequence of expounding its main theme'.

Another example of s 5 is the case of *Attorney-General* v *Times Newspapers*, (1987). The issue of the safety and security of the Queen was held to be a matter of serious public concern, and therefore the potential contempt arising from a discussion around whether an individual had had an affair with one of her police bodyguards was merely incidental to the discussion.

More recently, *The Observer*'s argument that an article it published which suggested that a lab technician on trial for stealing body parts was a necrophile was merely incidental to the article's wider discussion of necrophiliac and was not accepted in the Divisional Court. However, the article was not found to create a substantial risk to the course of justice, and the defence was not needed (see *Attorney-General* v *Guardian* (1999)).

✎ EXAM TIP

The defence of discussion of public affairs in s 5 can be a slippery concept to grasp, because the key concepts in it – 'good faith,' 'public interest' and 'incidental to the discussion' – can be open to wide interpretation. When answering a problem question, focus on including and discussing all of the elements, and don't worry too much about what conclusion you reach. Problem questions will not present you with a black/white scenario, so as long as you explain the defence, analyse the elements having regard to the case law and then apply it to the situation set out, you will get the marks. Improve your marks still further by tying the answer into the wider importance of freedom of expression.

Common law contempt of court

Section 6 of the CCA 1981 preserves common law contempt of court but restricts it to situations where the individual committing contempt *intends* to impede or prejudice the administration of justice. Under section 6(c) of the Contempt of Court Act 1981, it was up to the Attorney-General to prove beyond reasonable doubt that the publication (*actus reus*) in question by the defendants intended to impede or prejudice the due process of justice. It was enough if, in all circumstances, it could be inferred that the requisite interference took place, despite the newspapers' intention not to obstruct the proper course of justice, if it was virtually certain that it would do so. See below: *Attorney-General* v *Punch Ltd and Another* (2003).

KEY CASE

Attorney-General v *Punch Ltd* [2003] 2 WLR 49

Concerning: intention to impede or prejudice the administration of justice

Facts

David Shayler, the Middlesbrough FC fan and former MI5 agent, was accused of supplying information vital to national security to national newspapers. The Attorney-General started proceedings and Shayler and the newspapers were injuncted against further disclosures. Shayler subsequently wrote several articles for *Punch*, who was not a party to the injunction and the Attorney-General brought further proceedings against the magazine. The Court of Appeal held that the key was the purpose of the injunction, but disagreed over what the precise purpose was. In relation to *mens rea*, the court held that the *mens rea* of common law contempt required the editor of *Punch* to know that the publication would interfere with the course of justice by defeating the purpose underlying the injunction. If he misunderstood the purpose of the injunction, he would not have the relevant intention.

Legal principle

The Law Lords held that the focus of consideration should be on the court's purpose in making the injunction stopping Shayler from publishing. The court had intended to preserve the confidentiality of the material in the order. Therefore the editor of *Punch* knew that what he was doing interfered with this order, and this knowledge constituted intent for common law contempt purposes.

The requirement of proving intent means that common law contempt is little used; however, it is still applied in situations where proceedings are not active and so fall outside of the CCA 1981. Instead of the 'active' test, proceedings for common law contempt must be 'pending or imminent'.

> **!** Don't be tempted to . . .
>
> It is important that you understand the difference between 'active' proceedings under the Act, and the 'pending or imminent' conditions under the common law – the latter having been subject to varying judicial interpretations. In *Attorney-General* v *News Group Newspapers* (1988) Watkins J questioned whether the test was still necessary. Four years later, two judges in the Court of Appeal split on the issue: Bingham LJ holding the test was about 'imminence', and Hodgson stating that the key element was whether the proceedings were 'pending'. Beware of the question indirectly asking you to approach the problem under the Act and/or under the common law.

▉ In the jury room

The CCA introduced a blanket ban on release of any information from a jury. Under section 8 CCA 1981, obtaining, disclosing or soliciting the particulars of any statements made, opinions expressed, arguments advanced or votes cast by members of a jury in the course of their deliberations is a contempt of court.

The intention behind this wide-ranging ban is to protect the jury system, and despite the obvious conflict with freedom of expression it has been held to be rationally based and compatible with Article 10. However, it has been criticised by exponents of free speech and by academics and policy makers who are unable to research the quality of jury decision-making because of the ban.

Breaches of section 8 are taken very seriously, even where the intention of the individual breaching the rule was to avoid a potential miscarriage of justice. See, for example, the case of *Attorney-General* v *Fraill and Knox* (2011) where a juror used Facebook to converse with one of the defendants. She was sentenced to eight months' imprisonment. A recent example of the application of section 8 and the relationship between Article 10 and section 8 is the case of *Scotcher* in the House of Lords.

KEY CASE

Attorney-General v *Scotcher* [2005] UKHL 36

Concerning: s 8 of the Contempt of Court Act 1981

Facts

S was a juror in a case in which two boys were convicted. He felt the jury had not acted properly and wrote to the mother of the defendants setting out his numerous reasons. This letter was passed on to the police, and proceedings were brought against S for

---

contempt of court under section 8. Amongst other arguments, S argued that the desire to avoid a miscarriage of justice had to be a defence to a section 8 charge.

Legal principle

The House of Lords held that the desire to avoid a miscarriage of justice was no defence to an offence under section 8 and whilst S could have avoided a contempt charge if he had written to the court, writing to the mother of the defendants created all of the risks to the confidentiality of the jury's deliberations that section 8 was designed to avoid. Furthermore, section 8 was compatible with Article 10: the aim of upholding the jury system is an important one; the section itself is rationally connected to that aim and the means adopted by the section are no more than is reasonably necessary to protect the secrecy of jury deliberations.

Section 8 is backed up by a long-standing common law rule banning the admission of evidence of a jury's deliberations in any later action. The House of Lords considered this rule and its relationship with the right to a fair trial in *R* v *Mirza*; *R* v *Connor and Rollock* (2004).

Although deliberations in the jury room cannot be interfered with from external influences, including the court itself, nevertheless, discussion of the case in question by jurors may be open to scrutiny, where these discussions take place outside the confines of the jury room: for instance, in the corridors of the court, or inside the courts itself, or in a hotel in which the jury are staying overnight prior to returning to the jury room to consider their verdict, i.e. this would fall into the category of 'extrinsic' matters.

KEY CASE

R v *Young* [1995] 2 WLR 430

Concerning: matters outside of the jury room

Facts

This much publicised case involved the jury's verdict in a murder trial which was influenced by a ouija board, used by four jurors in a hotel room on the night prior to rendering their verdict in a murder trial. By using ouija board, the jurors asked and received answers from the murdered victims including the words 'Steven Young done it'. The appellant, Young, was subsequently convicted of a double murder. The appellant appealed on the grounds of a material irregularity, arguing that the jury's verdict was not solely based on the evidence given in court.

Legal principle

The court concluded that they could question the activities that went on at the hotel only (because that could not be considered to be 'in the course of their deliberations'), ▶

but not what transpired in the jury room later. They stated that what occurred in the hotel had to be considered as more than merely a light-hearted game and as a result was a material irregularity. The question was, did the jurors present believe the ouija board and was there a risk that they might be influenced by the answers given by the ouija? The court answered in the affirmative and allowed the appeal whilst at the same time ordering a retrial.

 Make your answer stand out

Any blanket rule lends itself easily to the sort of essay question which asks you to consider the pros and cons of the rule, because rules which do not allow discretion inevitably produce apparent injustices. In considering the secrecy of jury deliberations, better answers will see and criticise both sides of the argument, and tie in the right to a fair trial in Article 6, both in the specific sense of one individual and in the wider sense of the whole trial process.

In recent years problems have arisen with jurors searching the internet, in direct contravention of a judge's directions not to do so, in order to find out about extraneous matters relating to their trial, and, in many instances, to gather information about the accused. This has caused, and will no doubt continue to cause, considerable destabilisation of jury trials, if such behaviour is not suitably dealt with.

Sources of information

KEY STATUTE

Contempt of Court Act, s 10

No court may require a person to disclose, nor is any person guilty of contempt of court for refusing to disclose, the source of information contained in a publication for which he is responsible, unless it be established to the satisfaction of the court that disclosure is necessary in the interests of justice or national security or for the prevention of disorder or crime.

Section 10 CCA 1981 is designed to protect journalist's sources, a crucial aspect of media freedom since journalists regularly rely on tip-offs by individuals who do not wish to be identified. Section 10 was designed to liberalise the law and give more protection to the media but the courts have, until recently, applied the exceptions widely and given little credence to the value of protecting a journalist's source. The line of key cases on section 10 that you should consider in this particular are *X Ltd* v *Morgan Grampian Ltd* (1990); *Goodwin* v *UK* (1996); *Camelot* v *Centaur Communications* (1998); *Ashworth Security Hospital* v *MGN* (2002) *Mersey Care NHS Trust* v *Ackroyd (No. 2)* (2007).

KEY CASE

Interbrew SA v *Financial Times Ltd* [2002] EWCA Civ 274

Concerning: s 10 of the CCA

Facts

Documents relating to a potential takeover of a rival were leaked and Interbrew applied to the court to require disclosure of the documents in order to identify the source.

Legal principle

The court held that disclosure was required because of the damage to the business of Interbrew and their legitimate desire to identify who had leaked the documents, allied to the fact that it was not just confidential information but confidential and false information mixed in together. Since the appeal decision in March 2002, no documents relating to the disclosure have been delivered up to the claimants.

In November 2009 four national newspapers and Reuters complained to the European Court, under the name of *Financial Times Ltd* v *UK* (2009): application that the order to deliver up the documents to Interbrew constituted violations of, *inter alia,* Article 10. The court noted that, despite Interbrew knowing about the imminent publications, they did not legally seek to prevent any such publications. The court emphasised that a disclosure would only be justified 'in exceptional circumstances where no reasonable and less invasive alternative means of averting the risk posed are available' (at para 69). Despite Interbrew making alternative attempts to identify the source, sufficient evidence of these inquiries were not adduced as evidence before the domestic court. As a result, the court concluded that 'Interbrew's interests in eliminating, by proceedings against X, the threat of damage through future dissemination of confidential information .... were, even if considered cumulatively, insufficient to outweigh the public interest in the protection of journalists' sources' (at para 71).

 Make your answer stand out

Remember, the essence of s 10 of the CCA is to preserve the source's identity and any trail that may lead to 'outing' that person, usually via documents, records, discs, etc. Hence, there is a recognised and established strong presumption in favour of

▶

preserving the status quo of confidentiality. However, this presumption may be rebutted where the public interest establishes sufficiently compellable reasons to override the defendant's determination in retaining the confidentiality of the source's identity. Better answers will show that there are two public interests to be considered: the public interest in relation to protecting journalists' sources – an essential ingredient for freedom of expression – and the public interest in the administration of justice, disclosure being necessary (generally, in the interests of justice) as a pressing social need.

✎ EXAM TIP

Questions on s 10 require you to consider the important balance between freedom of expression, as demonstrated by press freedom to collect stories, versus the right to privacy. You will need to be able to explain and critique s 10 in this context, and consider the line of case law. Before *Ackroyd*, the courts favoured arguments of privacy over freedom of expression and in that context, *Ackroyd* could be seen either as a turning of the tide towards press freedom, or a single isolated decision. Crucially, it is vital to make clear the importance of the facts of the specific case: *Ackroyd* may well have been decided differently if there was a financial gain for the source or if the information had less public interest.

■ Publication of matters exempted from disclosure in court

The whole purpose of section 11 is based on the exceptions to the 'open justice' principles. Where the court possesses a power to make such orders which derogate from the normal open court principles, it should only do so if it appears that the due administration of justice will seriously suffer or be unworkable unless some form of action is taken to avert this.

■ Anonymity of witnesses

The withholding of a person's identity has been extended to witnesses appearing in court. Normally, for justice to be seen to be done, the defendant is entitled to see a witness, especially his accuser, giving evidence against him. This is a fundamental principle of the common law as well as under Article 6(3)(d) of the European Convention on Human Rights. Notwithstanding that, there may exist exceptional circumstances whereby a prosecution witness's identity should be withheld.

> **KEY CASE**
>
> *R* v *Davis* [2008] 3 WLR 125
>
> *Concerning: total witness anonymity*
>
> **Facts**
>
> The defendant had been charged with two counts of murder. The judge permitted the witnesses to give their evidence anonymously. Their testimony was crucial and embodied the sole evidence against the defendant (they could testify that the defendant was the gunman). As a consequence of the witnesses fearing for their own and their family's safety if they could be identified, the judge used his discretion and the witnesses' names, identity, addresses were withheld. The defendant was eventually convicted and appealed on the grounds that the 'protective measures' resulted in him not receiving a fair trial under Article 6 of the ECHR.
>
> **Legal principle**
>
> The House of Lords stated that, despite the witnesses being essential to the prosecution case, the fact that the defence were prohibited from recognising the witnesses nor being allowed to identify their voices constituted 'a significant potential detriment to the conduct of the defence'. In this particular instance these anonymity measures went beyond that which was considered appropriate for a fair trial. It is only in 'rare and exceptional circumstances' that the general rule will be put aside in favour of a judge's discretion to proclaim that certain protective measures will be introduced to shield a witness or victim from the defendant. Accordingly, the appeal was allowed.

■ Coroners and Justice Act 2009 (COJA)

The unsatisfactory position of the judgment of *R* v *Davis* led eventually to the Coroners and Justice Act 2009 (COJA). Part 3, Chapter 2 of the COJA deals specifically with the anonymity of witnesses. Prior to the court making a witness anonymity order, they must be satisfied as to the following conditions A–C as laid down in section 88(3)–(6).

> **KEY STATUTE**
>
> **Section 88 of the COJA**
>
> Under condition A the proposed order must be necessary (a) in order to protect the safety of the witness or another person or to prevent any serious damage to property, or (b) in order to prevent real harm to the public interest (section 88(3)(a) and (b)). Having regard to all the circumstances, the taking of those measures would be consistent
>
> ▶

with the defendant receiving a fair trial (Condition B of section 88(4)). In the interests of justice it is important that the witness should testify, and (a) the witness would not testify if the order were not made, or (b) there would be real harm to the public interest if the witness were to testify without the order being made (Condition C of section 88(5) (a) and (b)). Also, '[I]n determining whether the proposed order is necessary for the purpose mentioned in subsection (3)(a), the court must have regard (in particular) to any reasonable fear on the part of the witness – (a) that the witness or another person would suffer death or injury, or (b) that there would be serious damage to property, if the witness were to be identified' (section 88(6)). See *R* v *Powar (Harbinder Singh); R* v *Powar (Kulwinder Singh)* (2009).

Further, under section 89(1) and (2), prior to any order being made the court must have regard to a number of considerations. For a decision under the COJA, see *R* v *Alex Okuwa* (2010) where the court dismissed an appeal against a murder conviction, stating that despite the witnesses being permitted to give anonymity evidence the defendant had received a fair trial.

■ Putting it all together

Answer guidelines

See the essay question at the start of the chapter.

Approaching the question

- You should start with an introduction. Set the scene – what are the issues? Why is there a conflict between contempt of court and freedom of expression – define each briefly, and explain the nature of the conflict. Is it inevitable and why?

- You need to look at liability for contempt under both the CCA 1981 and the common law.

Important points to include

Your answer should cover the following issues and cases:

- S 1: strict liability; strict liability restricted by CCA to statutory contempt.

- S 2(2): elements of the statutory offence; key cases which define the aspects: e.g. *Attorney-General* v *English* (1982); *Attorney-General* v *MGN* (1997);*Attorney-General* v *MGN Ltd and News Group International Ltd* (2012).

- S 3, s 4, s 5: defences; key cases: *Attorney-General* v *English* (1982).
- Postponement orders; s 4(2).
- S 6: impact of common law; key cases: *Attorney-General* v *Sports Newspapers Ltd* (1991), *Attorney-General* v *News Group Newspapers Ltd* (1987), *Attorney-General* v *Hislop* (1991), *R* v *Thomson Newspapers ex p Attorney-General* (1968) – common law restricted to intentional contempt, but wider scope of application because of lack of 'active' period.
- S 7: role of Attorney-General.
- S 8: very broad ban on disclosure of jury information.
- S 10; key cases: *X* v *Morgan-Grampian* (1990), *Goodwin* v *UK* (1996), *Camelot* v *Centaur* (1998), *Ashworth Security Hospital* v *MGN* (2002), *Mersey Care NHS Trust* v *Ackroyd* (2007).

 Make your answer stand out

An excellent answer would show detailed understanding of principles, cases and context. Draw together the points you have made and answer the question asked – does contempt of court unfairly restrain the media? What are the deciding factors? Is the balance achieved the appropriate one?

READ TO IMPRESS

Brabyn, J. (2006) 'Protection against judicially compelled disclosure of the identity of news gatherers' confidential sources in common law jurisdiction', MLR 895.

www.pearsoned.co.uk/lawexpress

 Go online to access more revision support including quizzes to test your knowledge, sample questions with answer guidelines, podcasts you can download, and more!

Privacy and secrecy

Revision checklist

Essential points you should know:

- [ ] How privacy rights were protected under English law before the HRA came into force
- [ ] The effect of Art. 8's four rights and relevant Strasbourg cases on the domestic laws relating to privacy (and the problems caused by the lack of a single comprehensive privacy guarantee under English law)
- [ ] Post-HRA cases which have developed English law towards protection of privacy-related rights
- [ ] The rapid development of the law of breach of confidence into protection of 'reasonable expectation of privacy'
- [ ] That there is a necessary and difficult balance to be struck between privacy-related rights and freedom of expression/the public right of access to information
- [ ] The arguments for and against access to governmental information; the need to balance press freedom and the public right to know with national security interests
- [ ] The scope of freedom of information as a human right both in Strasbourg and under English law
- [ ] The key provisions and effect of the Official Secrets Acts (particularly the 1989 Act), and of the Freedom of Information Act 2000
- [ ] The principles under which equity will restrain publication of official information under public breach of confidence
- [ ] Current debates concerning privacy and secrecy

■ Topic Map

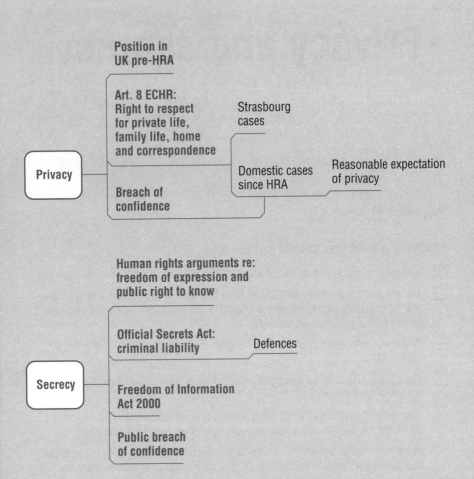

■ Introduction

Privacy is a complex and fast-evolving right in the United Kingdom.

The Human Rights Act is a major factor in that change, as are the decisions in cases since that statute came into force. The lack of a clear and coherent protection for privacy rights under English law has led to important cases both in domestic courts and in Strasbourg, and you must have a good understanding of these. It would be unwise not to have read the cases themselves, and a range of academic articles about them. This is also a chapter which interacts and overlaps with several others, making it equally unwise to attempt narrow revision or question-spotting! It is vital to keep up to date with case developments and reform proposals.

ASSESSMENT ADVICE

Even before the HRA came into force, privacy was a popular topic with examiners. However, old examination papers tended to focus upon the lack of a single, clear right to privacy under English law, or upon the contrast between Strasbourg and English cases on privacy rights. The law is changing very fast indeed here, and so it is vital that you stay up to date with relevant ECtHR and domestic cases. Both essay questions and problem questions are common.

Essay questions

A wide range of titles is possible in such a broad and dynamic field. Many questions require you to analyse how the law fits together here, whether domestic law or under the ECHR. For example, a question might ask you to compare how cases from the ECtHR and the UK uphold the rights protected by Art. 8; or whether English law still lacks protection for the right to privacy, or whether the HRA has cured the deficiencies of the previous English law in protecting privacy rights. 'Before and after' questions are quite often asked re the effect of the HRA: e.g. has the HRA led to a domestic right to privacy? But very specific questions are also possible, such as how courts have developed the right to respect for private life to encompass sexual autonomy or to restrict intrusive surveillance or to restrict intrusive journalistic practices. As always, it is vital to know what is on your syllabus and to assess how this topic was taught on your course!

Problem questions

It is becoming easier to ask problem-style questions on privacy rights, since there has been a rapid development in the relevant case law both in the UK and in Strasbourg. An examiner might set a scenario where the media are attempting to gain information

▶

about and/or photographs of a particular celebrity and ask you to assess the celebrity's chances of either preventing publication or obtaining damages after a publication. Obviously, you need to be up to date with recent domestic and ECtHR cases concerning privacy rights, including those where privacy arguments gave way to freedom of expression or other competing rights.

■ Sample question

Could you answer this question? Below is a typical problem question that could arise on this topic. Guidelines on answering the question are included at the end of this chapter, whilst a sample essay question and guidance on tackling it can be found on the companion website.

PROBLEM QUESTION

Luigi is a well-known male model and actor who has always had a high profile in the media, with many stories having been written about his public and private life. He has given interviews over the years in which he has talked about his strong relationship with his live-in girlfriend, Donna, and their desire to have children. He has just been contacted by *The Daily Maggot*, which is planning to publish the following about Luigi next week:

- a true account of his long affair with a 16-year-old girl last year;
- true details of his previous one-night-stands with several other women.

Luigi has previously denied that he had met any of these women, and threatened to sue for libel if any of the women went to the press with her story:

- an allegation that Luigi has had a vasectomy and is planning to leave his girlfriend;
- the terms of his advertising contract for a perfume brand;
- photographs of Luigi naked on holiday and of him leaving a sexual health clinic.

Advise Luigi as to his potential legal remedies, including his chances of preventing publication of the stories and photographs.

✎ EXAM TIP

Remember that privacy issues may crop up in problem questions which are largely about other human rights, e.g. in a police powers question or one on the rights of the media and the public right to know.

■ Privacy rights under English law before the Human Rights Act

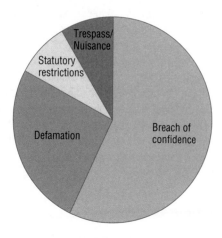

The above chart is not scientific, but is intended to represent the piecemeal and patchwork protection for privacy-related rights under domestic law before October 2000. You should know that, although England and Wales do not recognise a single legal right to privacy, 'privacy rights' have received increasing protection by the law, but that protection is patchy, incomplete and hidden within a large number of disparate laws. There is no single 'right to privacy', but rather a bundle of privacy-type laws which imply that some kind of right to privacy must exist. There is also no single concept of what 'privacy' means and, in contrast to many states, the UK has no constitutional protection for privacy. You should be able to discuss each of the main categories of privacy-protecting English law.

✎ EXAM TIP

You need to be aware of the historical reasons for the lack of a privacy law in England.

✔ Make your answer stand out

Show awareness of recent developments. A new defence of reportage is emerging in recent defamation cases, starting with *Reynolds* v *Times Newspapers* (1999), and protects responsible journalism. It protects 'the neutral reporting without adoption or embellishment or subscribing to any belief in its truth of attributed allegations of both sides of a political and possibly some other kind of dispute'. The House of Lords

▶

rejected an appeal application in *Roberts* v *Gable* in February 2008, signalling that public-interest publication is becoming a strong line of defence in defamation cases, with a consequent boost for freedom of expression. Then the Court of Appeal in *Flood* v *Times Newspaper Ltd* (2010) threw doubt (obiter) upon the scope of the defence, and appeared to limit the scope of the *Reynolds* responsible journalism defence. The Supreme Court heard an appeal in *Flood* in October 2011 but their judgment has not yet been published at the time of writing (January 2012), so keep an eye out for it. At the same time, the Supreme Court in *Joseph* v *Spiller* (2010) has rebranded the defence of 'fair comment' as 'honest comment' and made it easier to argue. Such defences are likely to be codified, and possibly expanded, in the expected statutory reform to defamation law in 2012–13. Quite how this will fit with the new privacy cases such as *Mosley* v *News Group Newspapers Ltd* (2008) is difficult to assess at present – freedom of expression and privacy are both developing rapidly, in opposite directions!

Statutory provisions

There is a wide range of statutes which have the effect of protecting aspects of privacy. The most important ones are in the following table.

> **□ REVISION NOTE**
>
> Again, don't forget to check your syllabus – did you spend a substantial amount of time in class on any of these statutes? If you did, then you obviously need to revise them thoroughly! Although almost every syllabus will include privacy, the range of approach, depth and detail between different courses is huge.

Statute	Relevant effect
Protection from Harassment Act 1997	Creates offences of 'stalking', i.e. a statutory tort of harassment where D knows or ought to know that his conduct will cause harassment, alarm or distress. Must be a 'course of conduct', not a single event.
Copyright, Designs and Patents Act 1988	Section 11: the copyright in a 'work' initially belongs to its 'author', unless the work was created by an employee who was acting in the course of his employment. Section 85: overrides the usual copyright of the person who takes a photograph so that a person who commissioned him to take it has the right to prevent it being published. A limited privacy right.

Statute	Relevant effect
Data Protection Act 1998	Schedule 1 sets out eight data protection principles which any 'data controller' must comply with when storing or processing personal information. The Information Commissioner has regulatory powers and deals with complaints. In *Campbell* v *Mirror Group* (2004) the argument of violation of the DPA failed, but in *Douglas* v *Hello! (No. 6)* (2006) the High Court did award small damages for breach of the DPA by publishing the photographs.
Regulation of Investigatory Powers Act 2000	Makes it a crime to conduct covert surveillance, such as telephone tapping, without authorisation. However, the Telecommunications (Lawful Business Practices) (Interception of Communications) Regulations 2000 authorise employers or government departments to intercept communications as long as 'reasonable efforts' have been made to inform employees of the possibility.
Police and Criminal Evidence Act 1984 and Codes of Practice	Limit police powers relating to stop, search, arrest, detention, interrogation; each of these has privacy implications. Some of the PACE rules have very obvious privacy angles, e.g. those regulating intimate searches and samples.

The problem: still not enough protection for privacy in the UK?

Article 8 has quite a broad scope, and cases have expanded its protection. Looking briefly at each of the four rights within the Article will demonstrate this. Remember of course that you need to cross-reference here with the discussion of Art. 8 in Chapter 2 of this book, and that the four rights overlap somewhat. As a reminder, each of the four rights may only be restricted where it is 'prescribed by law' and is 'necessary in a democratic society' in pursuit of a 'legitimate aim' from the list in Art. 8(2). It is especially important that the following steps be considered in order to decide whether a violation of Art. 8 has been shown:

1 Does the complaint fall within the rights protected by Art. 8?

2 Is there an infringement of these rights? If yes, then:

3 Under Art. 8(2), is this infringement justified, i.e. in accordance with the law? If yes, then:

4 Is the infringement within the legitimate aims stated in Art. 8(2), i.e. national security, prevention of disorder or crime, etc.? If yes then:

5 Were the measures taken by the public authorities 'necessary in a democratic society'? The word 'necessary' meaning a 'pressing social need' which was proportionate to the legitimate aim pursued. If yes, then:

6 The infringement is justified.

If the complaint falls within Art. 8's scope but there is no existing protection for his rights under English law, then there is an Art. 13 issue if the case goes to Strasbourg and the claimant can bring a free-standing HRA case (see Chapter 1).

Right to respect for private life

This includes the right to respect for your sex life and for sexual autonomy (*X and Y* v *Netherlands* (1985)), and can protect activities of a business nature since people spend so much time at work (*Niemietz* v *Germany* (1993)). Hence, surveillance of individuals may violate this right even when it is conducted on their office not their home (*Halford* v *UK* (1997)). A line of cases finds discriminatory criminal laws about sexual behaviour to violate Art. 8, for example *ADT* v *UK* (2001), *Sutherland* v *UK* (2001), but also note that such arguments failed in *Laskey, Jaggard and Brown* v *UK* (1997) where it was held to be legitimate in some circumstances for the state to regulate private sexual behaviour between consenting adults. Cases have also found it to be unjustifiable to prevent transsexuals from gaining legal recognition of their new gender (e.g. *Goodwin* v *UK* (2002)).

The right to respect for private life encompasses physical integrity, autonomy and dignity (*Costello-Roberts* v *UK* (1993)) and may prevent medical treatment without the patient's consent (*Glass* v *UK* (2004)). Cases have also dealt with abortion, the right to a name and the right to enjoyment of quality of life (*Pretty* v *UK* (2002)).

Right to respect for family life

The family life referred to here does not have to be a traditional one, and extends to a transsexual living with a long-term partner (*X, Y and Z* v *UK* (1997)). The removal of a newborn child from its mother for fear of abuse (*P, C and S* v *UK* (2002)) or the failure to allow a mother to challenge allegations that her partner had abused her child (*TP and KM* v *UK* (2002)) have been violations.

Right to respect for home

This category often overlaps with the previous two. In its own right, it protects from arbitrary eviction from or destruction of the home (*Gillow* v *UK* (1986)) but does not apply unless the applicant already has a home (*Buckley* v *UK* (1996)). Any local planning laws must not be discriminatory (*Connors* v *UK* (2004)). Disproportionate use of police powers may violate Art. 8 in this category (*McLeod* v *UK* (1995), *Keegan* v *UK* (2007)).

Right to respect for correspondence

This category overlaps with Art. 10's guarantee for freedom of expression; everyone has the right to communicate with other people. The right to respect for correspondence covers business telephone calls (*Halford* v *UK* (1997)) and regulates censorship of prisoners' mail (*Golder* v *UK* (1975), *Silver* v *UK* (1983)).

However, there is still a 'privacy gap' in English law, although it is shrinking since the HRA came into force.

KEY CASE

Wainwright v *UK* (2007) 44 EHRR 44

Concerning: privacy in the UK; the Art. 8 right to respect for private life

Facts

A woman and her disabled son were strip-searched by prison officers while visiting relatives in prison in January 1997 (thus before the HRA 1998 came into force in October 2000). They sued in trespass to the person and the House of Lords held that the HRA 1998 could not be used retroactively to create a right to privacy which had not

▶

existed at the time under the English common law. They brought a case to the ECtHR, arguing breaches of Arts 3, 8 and 13.

Legal principle

The court found a violation of Arts 8 and 13, but that the facts were not severe enough to reach the minimum threshold for Art. 3. Safeguards existed for ensuring that necessary searches of visitors to prisons would infringe their dignity as little as possible. Those safeguards had not been followed, leading to an Art. 8 violation (private life) and, since there had been no effective remedy in a domestic court, an Art.13 violation was also found.

A free-standing HRA claim would now be suitable on the facts.

KEY CASE

Peck v *UK* (2003) 36 ECHR 41

Concerning: private acts performed in public; the scope of Art. 8; lack of an effective privacy law in the UK

Facts

The applicant was spotted on CCTV wandering the streets of a city centre, covered in blood and holding a knife. It was thought that he might have committed a crime and so the CCTV footage was broadcast nationally. In fact he had attempted to commit suicide. There was no realistic chance of him enforcing his Art. 8 private life under English law and so he applied to the ECtHR.

Legal principle

The Strasbourg court found a violation of Art. 13 since Mr Peck had no effective remedy under domestic law for his argued Art. 8 violation. The reason why breach of confidence would at the time not give him a remedy for this was that his anguish was carried out in public and so did not have 'circumstances imposing an obligation of confidentiality'.

▉ Breach of confidence: towards a new privacy right in England and Wales?

The HRA 1998 has had a significant impact upon the principles of confidentiality. Breach of confidence is now the strongest protection under English law for privacy-related rights, and creates rights against intrusion whenever the claimant has a reasonable expectation of privacy.

Various limitations of the pre-HRA approach to confidentiality have been removed or changed in importance. It is thus crucial that you should be able to compare and contrast the law before and after the HRA.

 Make your answer stand out

Is breach of confidence the best claim to enforce privacy rights?

For a while in the 1980s and 1990s, it looked as if tort law would develop a new tort of invasion of privacy, but the case of *Hunter* v *Canary Wharf* (1997) signalled the end of that line. The House of Lords in *Campbell* v *Mirror Group* (2004) made the equitable doctrine of breach of confidence the new contender for a 'privacy law' and subsequent cases have developed its principles rapidly. But there are problems with this approach: as noted by the Consultation Paper, Lord Chancellor's Department (July 1993), *Infringement of Privilege*: 'the issue of breach of confidence cases is disclosure, while the issue of breach of privacy cases is publicity'. You can improve your marks by considering: would it have been better for the courts to create a new tort of invasion of privacy? Can breach of confidence continue to expand without causing problems for freedom of expression? See the 'Read to impress' section at the end of this chapter.

✎ EXAM TIP

There are many current legal developments which have an impact on privacy, and awareness of them may enrich your answers to many exam questions. For example, will the Leveson inquiry into phone-hacking lead to a different form of regulation for the media, who are often the defendants in privacy-related claims? What will be the final version of the new statutory reforms to defamation law?

The 'old' law of breach of confidence

Liability for breach of confidence under the 'old' law had a number of ingredients. The most important was that there was 'confidential information' which had the following elements:

1. wholly referred to information which is not in the public domain;

2. entrusted to an individual or a limited number of persons;

3. private in nature;

4. unauthorised disclosure strictly forbidden to the general public or a section of it.

There also used to be a requirement of a 'confidential relationship' between the confider and confidee, such as priest/penitent, solicitor/client, or one implied from marriage or business dealings, but this element was confirmed in *Campbell* to have disappeared some time before. In order to remind you briefly of the pre-HRA requirements for a successful confidentiality claim, the following table of key cases should help.

Case	Principle/effect
Prince Albert v *Strange* (1842)	Equity would intervene to grant an injunction prohibiting publication of the royal family's private etchings by the defendant, who had no property right in them and had obtained them in breach of confidence.
Schering Chemicals v *Falkman* (1981)	Business dealings between companies raised a presumption of confidentiality for information exchanged (note Lord Denning's dissent).
Coco v *Clark* (1968)	*Per* Megarry J, as between businessmen, in a business environment, with some eventual specific purpose, it would be difficult for a recipient to prove that the information he received was not meant to be confidential.
Argyll v *Argyll* (1967)	Breach of confidence is not restricted to contractual and commercial relationships; it applied to protect the secrets of a marriage since 'the confidential nature of the relationship is of its very essence and so obviously and necessarily implicit in it that there is no need for it to be expressed'.
Lennon v *News Group* (1978)	Where a marriage is an 'open book', it may contain no confidential information due to the publicity which the 'information' has already received.
Stephens v *Avery* (1988)	A lesbian affair could be 'confidential information' since couples in general regard their sex lives as not for public discussion. It, of course, would depend on the nature and the duration of the relationship. *Per* Browne Wilkinson V-C 'the basis of equitable intervention to protect confidentiality is that it is unconscionable for a person who has received information on the basis that it is confidential subsequently to reveal that information'.
Woodward v *Hutchins* (1977)	*Per* Denning MR, 'in these cases of confidential information, it is a question of balancing the public interest in maintaining the confidence against the public interest in knowing the truth'. On the facts, the plaintiff had sought to present a particular public image of himself and to use the media for PR, and so the balance lay in favour of publication. Some of the behaviour alleged to be confidential had also taken place in front of the public.

Case	Principle/effect
Khashoggi v *Smith* (1980)	Where the alleged confidential information includes allegations of iniquity, it is unlikely that an injunction will be granted under the law of breach of confidence. The plaintiff had also courted publicity, so 'ran the risk' of the story being made public.

Where the media decide to publish information, certain defences exist which may exempt them from any form of liability, and you should be familiar with them. The most used defence by the media when publishing controversial material is that it is in the 'public interest'. The exact meaning of those words are wide, uncertain and imprecise, but in essence the court must conduct a balancing exercise between two competing interests, as seen in *Lion Laboratories* (below).

KEY CASE

Lion Laboratories v *Evans* [1985] QB 256

Concerning: the public interest defence to breach of confidence

Facts

A newspaper published an article headed 'Exposed: The Great "Breath Test" Scandal', alleging that the Lion Intoximeter gave faulty readings, such that many drivers may have been wrongly convicted. The plaintiffs applied for and were granted an injunction restraining the newspaper from disclosing any confidential information about the device. The defendants appealed.

Legal principle

The appeal was granted. There were two competing public interests involved here: (1) the public interest of companies and the like to retain the secrecy of confidential information. That confidentiality should be maintained unless there is some justifiable reason existing which overshadows the continuance of privacy. (2) There are certain matters which not only are the public entitled to be informed about, but which also the media have a responsibility to report, 'even if the information has been unlawfully obtained in flagrant breach of confidence and irrespective of the motive of the informer'. The court said that such was the seriousness of the allegations, concerning as it did the lives and freedom of so many motorists (although there was no evidence of anyone being wrongly convicted) that it was in the public interest that the relevant documents be allowed to be published.

The 'new' law of breach of confidence: a privacy claim?

Almost immediately after the HRA came into force, there was a flurry of privacy-related claims brought under breach of confidence principles. Some of the useful ones are as follows (although we shall look more closely at *Von Hannover, Campbell* and *Murray* since they show important changes in approach).

Case	Principle/effect
Campbell v *MGN* (2004)	Where there was no prior relationship between the photographers and the claimant and no communication between them, the essentially private nature of the activity itself was enough to make it confidential. Breach of confidence is an action for misuse of private information.
Von Hannover v *Germany* (2005)	It is irrelevant to an Art. 6 private life claim that the applicant was in a public place when the photographs complained of were taken. *Von Hannover* v *Germany (No. 2)* was heard in the ECtHR in October 2010 but, at the time of writing, the judgment had not yet been published. Check for yourself whether it has by the time you are reading this, and note what the ECtHR held!
Douglas v *Hello! (No. 6)* (2005)	The requirements of breach of confidence have moved on since *Coco* v *Clark*: … 'knowledge, actual or implied, that information is private will normally impose on anyone publishing that information the duty to justify what, in the absence of justification, will be a wrongful invasion of privacy' (at 82) (note use of 'privacy'!).
A v *B* (2002)	A useful quote by Jack J: the law of breach of confidence is now, 'like a mother swollen with the child of privacy … given birth and the umbilical cord cut'.
McKennitt v *Ash* (2007)	A **'reasonable expectation of privacy'** is now the ground for a breach of confidence claim, not a confidential relationship.
Murray v *Big Pictures* (2008)	The Court of Appeal reversed trial judge's finding that there was no reasonable expectation of privacy for a celebrity's child being pushed in his pushchair in public.

Case	Principle/effect
Mosley v *News group Newspapers* (2008)	The publication of photographs of private S & M party without claimant's consent was an invasion of privacy. Eady J found that the claimant had a reasonable expectation of privacy for his consensual 'sexual activities (albeit unconventional)'.
	Mosley then took a case to the ECtHR, *Mosley v UK* (2011), arguing that the media should have to give advance notice to a person of publications that threatened to invade their privacy. He lost since a prior notification rule would have a chilling effect on freedom of expression. The Court also noted the existing remedies for breach of Art. 8 under English law and regarded them as adequate for Mosley's claim.

 Make your answer stand out

Tension between the courts?

This is a pivotal time in the development of breach of confidence into a privacy right. You should already know that Eady J gave key judgments in several of the above cases, which show the trend – it is worth reading them. But arguably these go beyond the House of Lords decision in *Campbell* and follow *Von Hannover*, a trend also seen in *Murray* v *Big Pictures* where the Court of Appeal reversed the trial court's original finding on the scope of protection for privacy. There has also been some backlash about 'super-injunctions' in cases such as *LNS v Persons Unknown* (2010). Until there is a Supreme Court decision confirming whether English law goes as far as *Von Hannover* in protecting ordinary and private things done in public, and until the decision in *Von Hannover (No. 2)* is available, there remains uncertainty about the eventual shape of breach of confidence and whether there is still a 'privacy gap' in English law. Excellent answers will discuss these issues.

KEY DEFINITION: Reasonable expectation of privacy

The requirement since *Campbell* (2004) for bringing a claim in breach of confidence/ misuse of private information. It depends on all the circumstances of the individual case.

In order to see how the new approach works in practice, let's finish the main body of this chapter by having a look at a few of the key recent cases in more detail.

KEY CASE

Campbell v Mirror Group [2004] 2 AC 457

Concerning: the new approach to breach of confidence after the HRA; reasonable expectation of privacy; misuse of private information; the confidentiality of photographs

Facts

The supermodel Naomi Campbell brought a breach of confidence action when photographs were published of her entering and leaving a Narcotics Anonymous meeting, accompanying stories which contradicted earlier statements she had made about drugs. She succeeded in the House of Lords (in a majority decision) in relation to the photographs but not the written information, since there was a public interest in the publication of the story to expose the truth.

Legal principle

The House of Lords decision is full of useful quotes and argument about the new role for breach of confidence in the human rights era. As stated by Lord Nicholls, 'This cause of action has now firmly shaken off the limiting constraint of the need for an initial confidential relationship' (at 13). So, breach of confidence now protects against publishing of private facts or pictures without authorisation; per Lord Nicholls, '... the law imposes "duty of confidence" whenever a person receives information he knows or ought to know is fairly and reasonably to be regarded as confidential' (at 14) and (eliding breach of confidence with Art. 8 actions), 'Essentially the touchstone of private life is whether in respect of the disclosed facts the person in question has a reasonable expectation of privacy' (at 21). The court labelled the action as one for 'the misuse of private information'.

KEY CASE

Von Hannover v Germany (2005) 40 EHRRI (ECtHR)

Concerning: the right to respect for private life under Art. 8 ECHR; whether Art. 8 protects activities carried out in public

Facts

Princess Caroline of Monaco was photographed in France carrying out her day-to-day life in public – collecting her children from school, shopping, and so on. The photographs were published in Germany. She brought claims in the German courts to enforce her Art. 8 right to respect for private life but failed since under German law she was treated as a public figure, meaning that the public had a legitimate interest to know how she behaved in public, even when she was not performing any official function. She brought an Art. 8 case to the ECtHR and won.

Legal principle

The ECtHR found unanimously that there had been an infringement of Art. 8, and that German law did not provide adequate protection for the right to private and family life.

The majority of the judges said that the question of the correct balance between Art. 8 and Art. 10 centres on 'the contribution that the published photos and articles make to a debate of general interest'. Since the photographs related solely to her private life and she had no official functions, there was no such 'contribution' on the facts. Thus, a clear 'public interest' is required to justify the publication of photographs of people who have no public function, even when those photographs are taken in public; non-consensual publication of pictures of ordinary occurrences in public can trigger Art. 8 liability (this was ruled out by Baroness Hale in *Campbell*). Arguably, therefore, *Campbell* still does not go far enough for this; the two cases were decided within days of each other, so there is some slight friction between them.

KEY CASE

Murray v *Big Pictures UK Ltd* (2008) EWCA Civ 448 (CA)

Concerning: the reasonable expectation of privacy; activities carried out in public; Art. 8, ECHR

Facts

JK Rowling's young son, in a claim brought by his parents, sought to prevent publication of covert long-lens photographs of himself taken when he was a toddler being pushed in his pushchair in the public street. The judge, Mr Justice Patten, dismissed the application for an injunction, stating that 'the law does not in my judgment (as it stands) allow them to carve out a press-free zone for their children in respect of absolutely everything'. On appeal, his decision was overturned.

Legal principle

According to the Master of the Rolls, Sir Anthony Clarke, 'If a child of parents who are not in the public eye could reasonably expect not to have photographs of him published in the media, so too should the child of a famous parent' unless the child's parents had already exposed him to the public eye. Thus, English law does seem to have moved towards the ECtHR decision in *Von Hannover*, so that non-consensual photographs of ordinary activities in public can be an 'invasion of privacy' or, more accurately, violate Art. 8 rights.

> ✎ **EXAM TIP**
>
> You should be able to explain and critique the effect of s 12(3) HRA 1998 in relation to the 'new' law of privacy in England and Wales; you should be familiar with how the section was interpreted in *Douglas* v *Hello!* and with the test adopted by the House of Lords in *Cream Holdings* v *Banerjee* (2004), for example. Section 12(3) requires that when a court is considering restraining freedom of expression via injunction, it should not do so unless satisfied that the applicant is likely to establish at trial that publication should not be allowed. The House of Lords in *Cream* interpreted 'likely' as meaning 'more likely than not', making prior restraint by injunction difficult to achieve in many cases. Note the distinctions drawn in the case of *LNS* v *Persons Unknown* (2010); where the injunction aimed to protect the claimant's commercial reputation rather than his privacy rights; freedom of expression prevailed and the injunction was lifted.

■ Official secrecy

In order for the public to be able to exercise their Art.10 'right to know' about the workings and actions of government, either they must be able to access government information directly or the media must be able to publish it. Hence, measures which prevent access to state information or restrict its publication raise human rights concerns. There is a delicate balance which is maintained between the citizen's right of access to information about the operation of government and the legitimate need of a state to withhold certain material from the public domain, at least temporarily. Those who work for the state may sometimes need to be able to disclose information to regulators, the media or the public without fear of criminal liability. You should understand the competing claims for secrecy and openness, and be able to evaluate the methods used to ensure secrecy and minimise the damage caused by breaches of confidentiality. In the light of the HRA and the Freedom of Information Act 2000, which came into force fully in 2005, some of the basic principles by which courts have upheld official secrecy require re-evaluation. It is now becoming increasingly difficult to justify the harshness of the offences under the Official Secrets Act 1989.

■ Arguments for and against official secrecy

You should be able to discuss these – see your textbook!

> 📖 **REVISION NOTE**
>
> Revise this topic with Art. 10 freedom of expression (discussed in Chapter 2 of this book): freedom of information is necessary in order to make some forms of expression, and the 'public right to know' is part of freedom of expression.

An example of how the competing rights are balanced in practice can be seen in *Stoll* v *Switzerland* (2007): there was a violation of Art. 10 where applicant had been fined for publishing a confidential state document concerning holocaust compensation. The ECtHR held that it had not been shown that the interests in favour of ensuring secrecy of the information were so important that they outweighed freedom of expression in a democratic society (but compare with *Leander* v *Sweden* (1987)).

📖 **REVISION NOTE**

Art. 10 compliance?

Even post-HRA, courts are arguably still interpreting the Official Secrets Acts offences with a great deal of deference for governmental views as to whether national security or state interests have been prejudiced by the defendants' actions: see *R* v *Shayler* (2002), below. Are such convictions really justified under Art. 10(2)? Look back at your notes on Chapter 2 if you need to be reminded of the requirements.

You should be familiar with the 1911 and 1920 Acts' scope and critique, and the cases of *R* v *Crisp and Homewood* (1919) and *R* v *Ponting* (1985). In short, the pre-1989 Acts were draconian, and had excessive and uncertain scope. The 1989 Act was a partial improvement but lacks a 'public interest disclosure' defence, which has again led to human rights concerns.

Liability under the OSA 1989

KEY DEFINITION: Damaging disclosure under OSA 1989, ss 1–4

'Damaging' means that the disclosure has damaged, or is likely to damage, one of the listed state interests in the relevant section.

The Official Secrets Act 1989 creates four main new categories of protected information, disclosure of which is a criminal offence:

■ Section 1 – information concerning security and intelligence;

■ Section 2 – defence;

■ Section 3 – international relations;

■ Section 4 – criminal investigations, including interception of communications.

For the s 1 offence, if the disclosure is made by someone who is or was in the security or intelligence services, or by a person who has been notified that he is subject to s 1, then there is no requirement for the disclosure to be 'damaging', but otherwise throughout the ss 1–4 offences it must be shown that the disclosure damaged, or was likely to damage, one of the listed state interests for the section charged. If you are allowed to take a statute book into your exam, you have an advantage in that you do not need to memorise the lists of **'damaging' disclosures** in each of ss 1–4!

For ss 1–4 only persons who are or have been members of the security or intelligence services, or who are or were Crown servants can be liable; there is also an offence under s 5 relating to disclosure of government information which was communicated in confidence, and this offence can be committed by any individual. There is an additional relevant offence under s 5 which covers e.g. media publication of information which they have received from a government employee.

The 1989 Act does not allow many defences, and those which do exist are relatively narrow in application. There are two defences which are created by the Act itself: first, a denial of the necessary mental state for conviction; and second, lawful authority. Other defences were considered at the White Paper stage but were rejected on policy grounds. A public interest defence was thought to be too difficult to apply due to the wide range of situations in which disclosure could be argued to be in the public interest, and it was also thought that the reforms in the 1989 Act would operate in such a way that only disclosures which were in fact contrary to the public interest would attract criminal liability. If this were so, then there was no need for such a defence. A general defence of prior publication was also rejected, it being thought that prior publication of the material in question would already be a factor to be considered in the assessment of whether the disclosure was 'damaging' and so did not require separate consideration. It was also argued that the fact that information has already been published elsewhere does not necessarily prevent the fresh disclosure from causing substantial damage, particularly if it adds weight to what was previously widely dismissed as gossip.

 Make your answer stand out

Re-evaluate these argued justifications for the 'missing' defences in the light of the HRA and Strasbourg cases on freedom of expression and national security. Have the following cases of *R* v *Shayler* and *R* v *Keogh* reached the right balance between secrecy and the right to know?

KEY CASE

R v *Shayler* [2002] UKHL 11 (HL)

Concerning: the human rights implications of the ss 1 and 4 offences under the Official Secrets Act 1989; whether a necessity defence applies to the Act

Facts

Re David Shayler, a preliminary ruling was made that there was no available defence of necessity, that there was also no public interest disclosure defence under either s 1 or s 4, and that both of those sections were compatible with Art. 10, ECHR. The Court of Appeal upheld this ruling; although it found that the defence of necessity might generally be available to such offences, it did not find any evidence that it applied on the present facts. The defendant appealed to the House of Lords on three grounds related to the availability and scope of defences to the offences charged.

Legal principle

Unanimously, the House of Lords held that although Art. 10, ECHR was engaged on the facts, ss 1(1) and 4(1) of the 1989 Act do not breach the Article because D did have a method by which he could make the whistleblowing disclosures lawfully to, e.g. the staff counsellor, the Attorney-General, the Director of Public Prosecutions, the police, the Prime Minister, various other ministers; hence the interference with his freedom of expression was proportionate to the legitimate aim of protecting national security. There is no public interest disclosure defence under the OSA.

But a more recent case had found a different human rights problem with the 1989 Act.

KEY CASE

R v *Keogh* [2007] EWCA Crim 528

Concerning: OSA 1989; reverse burdens of proof; HRA/ECHR

Facts

The facts of this case are lengthy and complicated and to summarise them here would add little to an understanding of the legal principle outlined below. Remember that examiners are usually looking for an understanding of the ratio and legal principle and that reciting the facts in an exam will not improve your grade.

Legal principle

Sections 2(3) and 3(4) of the OSA 1989 impose reverse burdens on D to prove that he has no knowledge and no reasonable grounds to believe that the disclosure he is making is damaging; the Court of Appeal used its HRA, s 3 powers to 'read down' the sections. The effect is that D will have a defence if he brings sufficient evidence to raise an issue as to his lack of *mens rea*; the state will then have to prove beyond reasonable doubt that D did not fall within the statutory defence.

■ Public breach of confidence

□ REVISION NOTE

We are now looking again at breach of confidence, which we studied earlier in this chapter. Where the claimant is the state, we shall refer to the action as 'public' breach of confidence for clarity's sake. Public breach of confidence has not yet evolved into a privacy-type action, unlike the other form.

In addition to the criminal liability under the OSA, civil measures are available in official secrecy cases through the use of the law of breach of confidence. In most situations where official secrecy is concerned, it is far more desirable to prevent any disclosure than to punish it once it has already occurred and caused damage. The civil law will not only operate to punish disclosure by way of an award of damages or another civil remedy; it is possible to obtain an injunction to prevent disclosure or publication of the secret information. As an exercise in damage prevention or limitation, the civil law may operate as a 'prior restraint' which prevents disclosure rather than simply an ultimate sanction, and may also confiscate any proceeds of the breach of confidence. However, unlike the Official Secrets Acts, there is a public interest publication 'defence' to breach of confidence actions.

 Make your answer stand out

Remember that prior restraint of expression via injunction raises an issue under s 12(3), HRA and Art. 10, ECHR, so you should be able to apply the House of Lords' 'more likely than not' test here from *Cream Holdings* v *Banerjee*. Obviously, national security can be a sufficient justification for prior restraint under both domestic law and the ECHR, but the balancing act must still be applied. Section 12(4) is also relevant.

Public breach of confidence can be represented as follows.

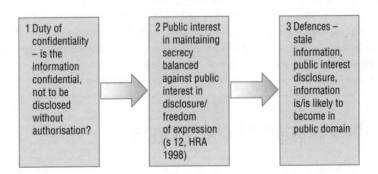

Although you have studied breach of confidence elsewhere, you should be familiar with at least the following cases on public breach of confidence.

Case	Principle/effect
Attorney-General v *Jonathan Cape* (1975)	Even pre-HRA, an injunction would only be granted if harm would be caused by the publication; so, where the information was 10 years old, the public interest in disclosure outweighed secrecy arguments.
Attorney-General v *Guardian (No. 2)* (1990)	Leading case on the public interest disclosure defence: applied *Lion Laboratories* v *Evans* test. Temporary injunctions preventing publication of Peter Wright's book, *Spycatcher*, were lifted since no continuing detriment to national security by publication could be shown once the book had already been published widely overseas. Hence, the public interest in freedom of expression outweighed secrecy. Once information is in the public domain, there cannot be a public interest in keeping it secret.
Attorney-General v *Blake* (2000)	Memoirs of an infamous spy were published; all profits from the book were confiscated and paid to the Crown, since Blake had profited through breaching his obligation to the Crown and it would be unconscionable for him to retain such profits.
Observer and Guardian v *UK* (1991)	Injunctions granted in the *Spycatcher* case before publication of the book overseas were a justified interference with Art. 10 rights, but those granted after that date were a disproportionate interference with freedom of expression since they could not have the aim of keeping secret information secret, hence, violation of Art. 10.
Blake v *UK* (2007)	ECtHR found that the decision in *Attorney-General* v *Blake* was sufficiently foreseeable to fit the 'prescribed by law' test and that the confiscation of profits was not a disproportionate interference with the right to enjoy his possessions (although the case took so long to go through the courts – 9½ years – that it did violate Art. 6!).
Attorney-General v *Times Newspapers, Kelsey and Leppard* (2001)	Tomlinson case: a good example of the balancing act post-HRA between the interests of secrecy and the public interest in publication. There had been a small amount of prior publication of the confidential material. Applying s 12(4), HRA and Art. 10, ECHR, the media role as public watchdog and communicator of public interest information to the public was referred to and no injunction was granted. It is for the state to demonstrate that there is a public interest in secrecy before an injunction will be granted; the defendant does not have to demonstrate that there has been prior publication overseas.
Attorney-General v *Punch* (2003)	The House of Lords confirmed that, once an injunction has been issued restraining publication of official information, it may be contempt of court to breach the injunction, and third parties may be liable for contempt in this manner.

! Don't be tempted to . . .

In Plural legal actions

You need to remember that there can be both criminal liability under OSA and civil actions at common law (prior restraint via injunction and actions for public breach of confidence). Both civil and criminal actions are often possible on the same set of facts (e.g. *Attorney-General* v *Blake*, *R* v *Shayler*) but of course the burden and standard of proof are much higher in a criminal trial. Make sure that you understand the difference between the forms of action and their effect for the defendant.

■ DA Notices – 'unofficial' official secrecy!

The methods of preventing or punishing disclosure of secret information which have been discussed so far in this chapter operate by way of civil or criminal law. DA (Defence Advisory) Notices, by contrast, are an extra-legal control upon disclosure by the media which operates entirely by goodwill and consent, albeit grudging consent and more often than not adhered to for fear of the alternative consequences. If you have covered DA Notices on your syllabus, you must be familiar with them.

Summary of the position so far

In summary, until 2000 the reforms to the criminal sanctions for disclosure of official secrets had made little difference to the overall system, which is still clearly characterised by an ethos of secrecy. Both criminal and civil sides to the issue assumed that official information should remain secret or confidential, unless there is a strong reason in favour of disclosure; this was supported further by the non-legal compliance structures, whether DA Notices or the needless practice of requiring all civil servants to sign a copy of the provisions under the Official Secrets Acts (which has no legal implications at all).

It is against this background that arguments arose, and gained strength, in favour of specific legislation to create a system of freedom of information. Such legislation is a common feature of many countries with written constitutions, and the present government made an election promise to introduce such legislation as a priority (although implementation of the legislation took some time). The basic principle of freedom of information legislation is that of a reversal of the previous secrecy ethos, with the result that it would be presumed that the public and the media should have free access to all government information, unless secrecy could be justified on public interest or other policy grounds, including of course national security.

■ The Freedom of Information Act 2000 – scope and effect

The Act, which came fully into force in 2005, creates a general right of access to information held by public authorities and limits the grounds upon which such access can be refused.

Section	Effect
Section 1: the general right of access to information held by public authorities	Any person can make a request for such information and has the right to be informed in writing whether the authority holds such information and, if it does, the right to have it communicated to him.
Section 10: timing	Public authority must comply with request within 20 days (although it can request further information under s 1(3) and can delay for non-payment of fees).
Section 17: reasons for refusal	If the public authority refuses the request because the information is exempted, it must state the exemption relied upon when giving reasons for refusal of the request.
Sections 21–44: exempt information	There is a very long list of exempt information, i.e. grounds upon which it is legitimate to refuse a request for information. Grounds include: ■ where the information is reasonably accessible by other means; ■ where the public authority intends to publish the information in future; ■ where the subject matter of the requested information is sensitive for one of many reasons, including that it relates to national security, criminal investigations, court records, government policy, personal information, health and safety, privately or commercially confidential information … the breadth of the exemptions thus limits the effect of the Act greatly.
Sections 51–59: enforcement procedures	There is a right to complain to the Information Commissioner (IC) if a request is not dealt with in accordance with the Act. The IC has powers to obtain information from the public authority, and to issue a 'decision notice' and 'enforcement notice'. There is a right of appeal to the Information Tribunal. Failure to comply with the IC's requests and 'notices' may be treated as contempt of court.

Make your answer stand out

Depending on your syllabus, you may need to discuss relevant cases which interpret the provisions of the Freedom of Information Act. For example, *Common Services Agency* v *Scottish Information Commissioner* (2008) on the scope of 'personal data' under s.40; *Sugar* v *BBC* (2010) on the exemption for information held for the purposes of journalism, art or literature, and on the appeal process. If you covered the Act in any detail, you need to be able to demonstrate detailed understanding of relevant cases.

Advantages of the 2000 Act over the previous Code of Practice

The advantages include:

- A statutory right of access to information has been created for the first time in the UK.

- A far more comprehensive range of public authorities are covered by the new Act.

- The new Information Commissioner is directly accessible to members of the public, whereas under the Code the intervention of a Member of Parliament was necessary; the enforcement mechanism for the Act is far stronger than its predecessor.

- The right of access is to the original documents, or copies thereof, rather than to the information contained therein.

- The Public Records Act 1958 has been substantially amended to allow for access to documents governed by that scheme, subject to exceptions.

- Although the exemptions under the 2000 Act are still very broad, they are generally less extensive than those which existed under the Code.

✎ EXAM TIP

The Freedom of Information Act is a relatively new and important piece of legislation so it is in your interests to be able to discuss and evaluate it and the role of the Information Commissioner.

It might also be helpful to be able to compare and contrast its provisions against those of other jurisdictions – Canada and the USA are good examples for freedom of information regimes. There is a further practice question on the supporting website.

■ Putting it all together

Answer guidelines

See the problem question at the start of the chapter.

Approaching the question

A question on breach of confidence and privacy, which requires systematic use of a plan and headings.

Important points to include

- Key issues include the availability of prior restraint and the application of s 12 of the HRA 1998, the requirements of an action for breach of confidence and the extent to which there is now a right to privacy against media intrusion.

- You need to show that you understand and can apply recent authorities including *Campbell*, *Von Hannover*, *A* v *B*, *H R H Prince of Wales* v *Associated Newspapers Ltd* (2008), *McKennitt*, *Murray*, and *Mosley*, as well as explaining the continuing relevance of some elements of the 'old' law of confidence. There is an issue of commercial confidentiality (advertising contract) and one of notoriety/hypocrisy. The photographs deserve separate consideration of *Peck*, *Campbell* and *Von Hannover*.

> ✓ Make your answer stand out
>
> As always, detailed application of relevant and recent cases, showing that you have read them and read articles about them, will make a big difference to the quality of your answer. This would enable you, for example, to distinguish whether English law is still different from the relevant Strasbourg cases, and whether different rules apply to photographs and written publications. A good answer will refer to the need to balance the rights and needs of the press (including the public right to know) against privacy-related rights.

READ TO IMPRESS

Brazell, L. (2005), 'Confidence, privacy and human rights: English law in the twenty-first century' EIPR 40.

Chadwick, P. (2006), 'The value of privacy' EHRLR 495.

▶

Millar, G. (2009), 'Whither the spirit of Lingens?' EHRLR 277

Schreiber, A. (2006), 'Confidence crisis, privacy phobia: why invasion of privacy should be independently recognised in English law' IPQ 160.

www.pearsoned.co.uk/lawexpress

 Go online to access more revision support including quizzes to test your knowledge, sample questions with answer guidelines, podcasts you can download, and more!

Obscenity

7

Revision checklist

Essential points you should know:

- [ ] The significance of the ECHR in this context

- [ ] The main arguments for and against regulation of extreme 'speech', including pornography

- [ ] The 'obscenity' offences under the Obscene Publications Act 1959 and the 'extreme pornographic image' offence under the Criminal Justice and Immigration Act 2008, including critique of all applicable offences

- [ ] The general significance of other laws that also regulate specific aspects of obscenity and 'indecency

■ Topic Map

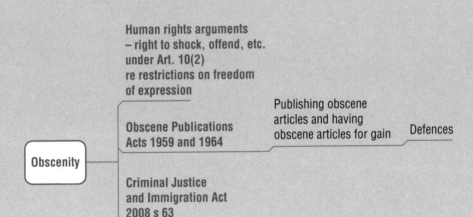

**Human rights arguments
– right to shock, offend, etc.
under Art. 10(2)
re restrictions on freedom
of expression**

**Publishing obscene
articles and having
obscene articles for gain**

Defences

**Obscene Publications
Acts 1959 and 1964**

Obscenity

**Criminal Justice
and Immigration Act
2008 s 63**

A printable version of this map is available from **www.pearsoned.co.uk/lawexpress**

■ Introduction

The recent introduction of legislation regulating 'extreme pornographic images' has revitalised the debate concerning free speech and the law on obscenity and related offences.

In the well-known '*Lady Chatterley's Lover* case', *R* v *Penguin Books Ltd* (1961), the Chief Prosecutor asked members of the jury to consider whether they would approve of their wife or servants reading the allegedly obscene book in question. Given this antiquated prosecution view of society in general and the lives of jury members in particular, it is not surprising that the law on obscenity and similar offences is frequently seen as outdated and inappropriate. Many of its rules have changed little, if at all, in decades, and there are generally fewer than 100 prosecutions per year under the Obscene Publications Act (although there are thousands for child pornography offences). The introduction of an offence concerning 'extreme pornographic images' has revitalised the debate regarding the regulation of extreme images and free speech in this context and strengthened the controls on the possession of sexually explicit material.

ASSESSMENT ADVICE

Students must display an understanding of the OPAs 1959 and 1964. They must also be familiar with other important relevant legislation, such as the Criminal Justice and Immigration Act 2008, and other pertinent UK laws and ECHR jurisprudence in this area. Examination questions often focus on new developments in the law; this topic is no exception.

Essay questions

These frequently require you to assess the validity of domestic laws regulating obscenity and indecency. They questions require you to critically analyse the relevant legislation and case law and consider whether they strike an appropriate balance between free speech norms and other objectives, such as the prevention of harm or the protection of public morals. In considering these questions, you must provide a clear, succinct and accurate outline of the main laws, as interpreted by the domestic courts and the ECtHR. You must also carefully consider the arguments for and against the laws in question; it would be an error for you to focus on one side of the argument, and to appeal to emotion. You need to examine the arguments in a dispassionate manner, and to back up your discussion with reference to relevant academic commentary, case law and statute law.

▶

Problem questions

Those concerning obscenity and indecency are likely to be similar to general criminal law questions: you will need to consider whether an offence has been committed, which will require you to begin by considering the elements of the offence. You will need to refer to relevant legislation and case law, and to explain how you reached any conclusions about particular issues. The examiner will be interested in your understanding of the relevant laws, as demonstrated by your explanations; you will need to discuss any arguments for and against liability. Your answers should follow a clear, logical structure; in this respect, you might find it useful to use headings and sub-headings. The best answers will spend more time on contentious or complicated matters, but they will demonstrate an awareness of every issue raised by the question.

■ Sample question

Could you answer this question? Below is a typical essay question that could arise on this topic. Guidelines on answering the question are included at the end of this chapter, whilst a sample problem question and guidance on tackling it can be found on the companion website.

ESSAY QUESTION

To what extent is there a right to shock and offend under English law and the ECHR? Is the current law satisfactory in this respect?

■ Background

Until 2008, there were no English criminal offences dealing specifically with pornography, although there were criminal laws governing '**obscene**' and 'indecent' articles and displays. The Criminal Justice and Immigration Act 2008 now makes it an offence to be in possession of an 'extreme pornographic image', but it does not regulate pornography generally. This Act also increased the maximum penalty for publication of obscene material and for the possession of such material for gain under the Obscene Publications Act 1959, and thereby strengthened the regime controlling obscene material. The 1959 Act (as amended by various statutes, including the Obscene Publications Act 1964) remains one of the main statutes governing sexually explicit material, but there many other relevant statutes in this context: these include the Protection of Children Act 1978, the Indecent Displays (Control)

Act 1981, the Malicious Communications Act 1998, the Postal Services Act 2000, and the Communications Act 2003. There are also two notable common law offences in this context: outraging public decency, and conspiracy to corrupt public morals (see *Knuller (Publishing, Printing and Promotions) Ltd v DPP* (1973).

> **✎ EXAM TIP**
>
> The Obscene Publications Act 1959 and the Criminal Justice and Immigration Act 2008 are of central importance here. You should check your syllabus to determine which other offences are important in the context of your exam.

■ The Obscene Publications Act 1959

KEY STATUTE

> **OPA 1959, s 2(1)**
>
> Under s 2(1), it is an offence to publish an 'obscene article for gain or not' or to have an obscene article for publication for gain.

You need to know that 'article' has a wide definition under this Act, and that it means anything 'containing or embodying matter to be read or looked at or both, any sound record, and any film or other record of a picture or pictures' (s 1(2)). Similarly, it is crucial that you know publication has a wide definition under the Act, and that electronically transmitting data via the internet constitutes a publication (s 1).

> **✎ EXAM TIP**
>
> Examination questions in this area may focus on the application of the law to the internet. Essay questions may ask you whether domestic laws can deal with obscenity and indecency effectively and fairly in the 'internet age', given jurisdictional issues where the material in question originates in another country. Similarly, problem questions may ask you about the application of the Obscene Publications Act 1959 and related legislation to a website accessed in England but located in another jurisdiction. *R v Perrin* (2002) is an important case in this context, since it assumes that the viewing of a web page in England is a publication by the defendant in this country even if the website is located in another jurisdiction.

KEY DEFINITION: Obscene

> An article is obscene 'if its effect or (where the article comprises two or more distinct items) the effect of any of its items is, if taken as a whole, such as to tend to deprave and corrupt persons who are likely, having regard to all relevant circumstances, to read, see or hear the matter contained or embodied in it'.

At common law, it was not necessary for the prosecution to establish that the defendant's motive was to deprave and corrupt (*R* v *Hicklin* (1868)). The courts take a similar approach under the 1959 Act (see *R* v *Penguin Books* (1961)). Thus, the Court of Appeal has held that 'obscenity depends on the article and not upon the author' (*Shaw* v *DPP* (1962)).

❗ Don't be tempted to . . .

You need to be clear about when intention is relevant to the test for obscenity. The effect of the article determines whether it is obscene but this does not mean that the intention of its creator *as perceived by likely readers or viewers* is irrelevant. If a book graphically describes a 'depraved' or 'corrupt' lifestyle in what seems to be a condemnatory manner, the perceived tone of the book may be relevant in determining whether it has a tendency to deprave or corrupt: by adopting an apparently condemnatory attitude, it may discourage likely readers from pursuing the lifestyle.

KEY CASE

R v *Anderson* [1972] 1 QB 304

Concerning: the test for obscenity under the Obscene Publications Act 1959

Facts

The 'Oz School Kids Issue' led to charges under s 2, OPA.

Legal principle

A magazine or equivalent article is obscene if one distinct part of it is obscene; the issue is whether the article in question has a tendency to deprave and corrupt, not whether it is 'repulsive', 'filthy', 'loathsome' or 'lewd'.

KEY CASE

DPP v *Whyte* [1972] AC 849

Concerning: the test for obscenity under the Obscene Publications Act 1959

Facts

The issue was whether the books and magazines sold by the defendants in their shop were obscene. The defendants advanced two main arguments. First, they claimed that the material was not obscene because it would enable their customers to engage in private fantasies, but it would not influence their sexual conduct with other people.

Second, they claimed that their regular customers were in any case 'addicts of this kind of material, whose morals were already in a state of depravity and corruption', and that the material could therefore not deprave or corrupt them.

Legal principle

The House of Lords found that the defendants had contravened the Act. Their Lordships stated that 'influence on the mind is not merely within the law but is its primary target', and that, therefore, it is not necessary for the prosecution to show that the material tends to have an effect on conduct. Furthermore, they held that the Act 'protects the less innocent from further corruption, [and] the addict from feeding ... his corruption', and that it accordingly applies to articles that maintain a state of corruption.

 Make your answer stand out

You can improve your exam performance by emphasising that the primary purpose of the Act is to protect the minds of those who are likely to encounter the article, and that the Act does not focus on the harm that 'corrupted' or 'depraved' individuals might inflict on other people.

Defences

There is a 'no reasonable cause to suspect that the article is obscene' defence in s 2(5) of the 1959 Act but this defence has an extremely restricted meaning. Section 1(3)(a) of the 1964 Act provides an equivalent defence relating to a charge of 'having an obscene article for publication for gain'.

KEY DEFINITION: Public good

Section 4(1) of the 1959 Act creates a 'public good' defence: it stipulates that a defendant shall not be liable 'if it is proved that publication of the article in question is justified as being for the public good on the ground that it is in the interests of science, literature, art or learning, or of other objects of general concern'. The Act stipulates that this defence does not apply 'where the article in question is a moving picture film or soundtrack', but there is a similar defence in relation to such an article where 'the publication ... is justified as being for the public good on the ground that it is in the interests of drama, opera, ballet or any other art, or of literature or learning' (s 4(1A)).

The **'public good'** defence is only relevant when the jury has determined that the article is obscene. Section 4 places the onus on the defendant to establish that the publication is probably for the public good.

R v *Calder & Boyars Ltd* [1969] 1 QB 151

Concerning: the 'public good' defence under the Obscene Publications Act 1959

Facts

The defendants were charged with having published an obscene book, *Last Exit to Brooklyn*. They argued that it was not obscene because it would deprave only 'a minute lunatic fringe of its readers', and furthermore claimed that the publication was in any case justified as being for the public good in accordance with s 4.

Legal principle

An article is not obscene if 'the only effect that it would produce in any but a minute lunatic fringe of readers would be horror, revulsion and pity'. The jury should consider the potentially harmful effect of the material: that is, the numbers of people who would tend to be depraved and corrupted by the article, the strength of the tendency, and the nature of the depravity or corruption. They should then balance this against 'the strength of the literary, sociological or ethical merit' of the article, and determine whether the publication is on balance for the public good.

The Obscene Publications Act 1964

You need to be aware that this Act amended the OPA 1959 in various respects, in particular to make it an offence to have an obscene publication **for gain**.

It is clear that the gain in question does not have to be for the defendant; 'gain for another' is sufficient (Obscene Publications Act 1959, s 2(1), as amended by the 1964 Act). However, the legislation does not define 'gain'. Financial benefit will count, but other sorts of gain, such as the receipt of pleasure derived from the article, may also suffice.

The ECHR and the HRA

Article 10(1) of the ECHR stipulates that everyone has the right to freedom of expression, and the HRA makes special reference to the importance of the right to freedom of expression, s 12 of which stipulates that 'the court must have particular regard to the importance of the Convention right to freedom of expression'. However, Art. 10(2) makes it clear that this right can be subject to certain necessary restrictions: for example, 'for the prevention of disorder or crime' or 'for the protection of health and morals'. The issue in this context is whether the restriction is necessary and proportionate under Art. 10(2). The domestic courts and the ECtHR have often found that interferences with the right to freedom of expression are justified, or acceptable, in this way. Nonetheless, the ECtHR has also held that freedom of expression is important where the contribution of the press to matters of public interest is at stake.

📖 REVISION NOTE

You should revise this topic alongside the ECHR chapter. You should be prepared for overlaps with Strasbourg cases: they may be relevant in multiple contexts; for example, a case concerning Art. 10 could have implications for obscenity law even if the facts of the case concerned defamation.

✎ EXAM TIP

A key point to make about the law on obscenity is its potentially wide application. There is uncertainty about what counts as 'depravity' and 'corruption' in this context. Given the vagueness of these notions, the law can be criticised for lacking sufficient precision to satisfy the principle of fair warning. If a person cannot know what will break the law, he or she may remain silent rather than risk prosecution. If relevant, you should emphasise that this has implications for the right to freedom of expression. However, you will obtain higher marks if you also point out that other Convention rights are at issue here: for example, Art. 7, which provides that there should be no punishment without law.

KEY CASE

R v *Perrin* [2002] EWCA Crim 747

Concerning: the Obscene Publications Act 1959 and the right to freedom of expression

Facts

The defendant published an obscene web page on the internet. He relied on Arts 10 and 7 in his defence.

Legal principle

The Court of Appeal upheld the defendant's conviction. It held that the law on obscenity was sufficiently precise, since the Act gives 'the word "obscene" a restricted meaning which is more demanding than its dictionary meaning'. Furthermore, it found that 'Parliament was entitled to conclude that the prescription was necessary in a democratic society'.

✎ EXAM TIP

You can impress examiners by considering the correct interpretation of Art. 10(2) by domestic courts. *R* v *Perrin* (2002) suggests that Parliament has a margin of appreciation under the HRA in determining whether a prescription is necessary: the Court of Appeal's decision in this case implies that the issue is not whether a prohibition is necessary in a democratic society, but whether Parliament was 'entitled to conclude' that it is necessary. Commentators generally argue that the 'margin of appreciation' doctrine should have no place in the domestic interpretation of Convention rights.

KEY CASE

Hoare v *UK* [1997] EHLR 678

Concerning: the Obscene Publications Act 1959 and the right to freedom of expression

Facts

The applicant sold obscene videos in a national newspaper, and was convicted of s 2. Before the European Commission of Human Rights (First Chamber), he argued that the state had unjustifiably interfered with his freedom of expression contrary to Art. 10. He admitted that the video tapes were obscene under the 1959 Act, but claimed that the restriction of his freedom of expression was disproportionate, since he only distributed the articles to people who expressed a clear interest in them.

Legal principle

The European Commission rejected the application. It stated that there must be 'particularly compelling' reasons to justify an interference with the Art. 10 right in a case like this 'where no adult is confronted unintentionally or against his will with filmed matter'. However, it found that the applicant's conviction had been justifiable. Although it accepted that the video tapes were unlikely to be purchased accidentally, it held that they could nonetheless be viewed by others, including minors. The video tapes had no artistic merit, and the applicant had no control over them once they left his hands. This meant that the applicant's conviction for publishing them 'was not disproportionate to the legitimate aim pursued'.

KEY CASE

Handyside v *UK* (1976) 1 EHRR 737

Concerning: the Obscene Publications Act 1959 and the right to freedom of expression

Facts

The applicant was convicted under s 2(1) re *The Little Red Schoolbook*, intended for schoolchildren aged 12 years and older and containing advice about various issues, including sexual matters. He made two main arguments before the ECtHR: first, that the UK had infringed his Art. 10 right; second, that the UK had also violated his right to the peaceful enjoyment of his possessions under Art. 1 of Protocol No. 1. In relation to these points, the applicant stressed that the majority of the member states of the Council of Europe had not sought to prohibit the book.

Legal principle

The court rejected the application. It found that the relevant UK statute legitimately aims to protect morals, and that the action in question had been necessary to promote this legitimate objective. The court decided that the fact that other member states allowed the work to be distributed did not mean that the UK had breached Art. 10. As the court put it, member states have a margin of appreciation, and the UK had acted within its discretion, since the English court had been entitled on the facts to conclude that the book 'would have pernicious effects on the morals of many of the children and adolescents who would read it'. Having found that the action against the applicant was necessary for the protection of morals, the court concluded that this action had been justified under Art. 1 of Protocol No. 1 as being in the public interest.

 Make your answer stand out

Show awareness of recent developments. There are very few prosecutions under the OPA these days, and a recent case has led to calls for the Crown Prosecution Service to rethink their guidance on the kinds of content which justify prosecution in modern society. Peacock was acquitted on 6 January 2012, which indicates that prosecutors may be out of step with juries' beliefs as to what is capable of 'depraving and corrupting' by today's standards. It is only a first instance decision so watch out for any further cases, but it does appear that juries are broader-minded than the OPA is about pornography. It is likely that there will be calls for the abolition of the OPA offences, but retention of the child pornography and extreme pornography offences.

■ The Criminal Justice and Immigration Act 2008

This Act stipulates that it is an offence to be in possession of an 'extreme pornographic image' (s 63(1)).

KEY STATUTE

Criminal Justice and Immigration Act 2008, s 63

The definition of an 'extreme pornographic image' is complex. An image is 'pornographic' if it is of such a nature that it must reasonably be assumed to have been produced solely or principally for the purpose of sexual arousal' (s 63(3)). It is 'extreme' if it explicitly and realistically portrays specific matters, such as certain violence, and 'it is grossly offensive, disgusting or otherwise of an obscene character' (s 63(6) and s 63(7)).

 Make your answer stand out

Excellent answers may discuss the rationale of the extreme pornography offence. What harm(s) is it designed to prevent? Does it take a different approach to the 1959 Act? You should also consider whether the new offence is consistent with the Art. 10 right to freedom of expression and other Convention rights. See the articles by Rowbottom (2006) and McGlynn and Rackley (2007).

The extreme pornography offence does not apply to BBFC classified films (s 64(1)). However, this exemption pertaining to classified works does not cover situations where an image from a classified work is 'extracted ... solely or principally for the purpose of sexual arousal' (s 64(3)). There are general defences (s 65). The burden of proof is on the defendant in relation to these defences. First, there is a defence if the accused had 'a legitimate reason for being in possession of the image concerned'. Secondly, there is a defence if the defendant shows that he or she 'had not seen the image concerned and did not know, nor had any cause to suspect, it to be an extreme pornographic image'. This defence is similar to the 'no reasonable cause to suspect' defence under the 1959 and 1964 Acts, and the courts will presumably interpret it in the same limited manner. Thirdly, there is a defence pertaining to an unsolicited image that is not kept by the defendant 'for an unreasonable time'. There is an additional specific defence for those who participate in the creation of extreme pornographic images, but this defence is of limited application and the burden of proof is again on the defendant (s 66).

Obscene Publications Act 1959	Criminal Justice and Immigration Act 2008
Makes it an offence to publish an obscene article or have such as an article for publication for gain	Makes it an offence to be in possession of an 'extreme pornographic image'
Applies to articles generally	Only applies to images

Obscene Publications Act 1959	Criminal Justice and Immigration Act 2008
Designed to prevent depravity and corruption of the minds of those likely to encounter the article	Arguably informed by a 'harm to women' perspective
Defences:	Defences:
■ 'no reasonable cause to suspect' ■ public good	■ no reasonable cause to suspect' ■ legitimate reason for possession ■ unsolicited image ■ participation

 Make your answer stand out

There have been over 1000 prosecutions under the new extreme pornography legislation, which was introduced with a promise that it would not lead to an increase in prosecutions and would not criminalise behaviour which was not already unlawful! Several of the cases have hit the headlines due to either sensational facts or controversial applications of the law, and it is in your interests to know about them if the 2008 Act is on your syllabus. For example, *R* v *Day* (2010) *R* v *Rollason* (2010) and *R* v *Cox* (2009) would clearly have been guilty under the prior law, but *R* v *Heard* (2010) and *R* v *Holland* (2010) (the tiger case) are both cases which raise concerns about fairness and appropriate charging. *R* v *Dymond* (2010) (the dead squid case) also has some challenging aspects.

■ Putting it all together

Answer guidelines

See the essay question at the start of the chapter.

Approaching the question

You need to start by defining the elements of the question: what are the main offences in this context? What are the relevant Convention rights? You need to explain that you will consider the right to shock and offend in the context of the domestic law on obscenity and other significant offences, and that you will consider pertinent domestic and ECtHR decisions on Convention rights. You should make it clear that you will begin by outlining the relevant law, and that you will then assess the adequacy of this law in the light of academic and other debate.

Important points to include

You should outline the way that the 1959 and 2008 Acts deal with shocking or offensive articles and images; for example, you should consider the scope of the s 2(1) offence under the 1959 Act. You should explain the scope and application of these Acts and other offences to shock and offend. You should also consider the way that courts have applied the ECHR in this context. Finally, you should consider the arguments for and against the current law and reach a conclusion about its appropriateness.

 Make your answer stand out

The way to really stand out and impress examiners is to explain how you reached your conclusions. It is not enough to reach a clear conclusion, or to state your argument in a forthright manner. As we said above, you must consider both sides of the debate with careful reference to the law. Questions on this area are very popular with students. A typical mistake in this context is to believe that you do not need to outline fundamental rules and principles and consider their application by the courts because 'everybody knows' about these matters. In fact, you do need to discuss these basics, such as the test for 'obscenity' under the 1959 Act, in order to display your understanding of them. You also need to display a strong understanding of the underlying basis of the human rights at stake, and to tie this knowledge in to your discussion.

READ TO IMPRESS

Livingstone, S. and Millwood Hargrave, A. (2006) '*Harm and offence in media content: a review of the evidence*'. Bristol: Intellect Books.

McGlynn, C. and Rackley, E. (2007) 'Striking a balance: arguments for the criminal regulation of extreme pornography', Crim LR 677–90; and (2009) 'Criminalising extreme pornography: a lost opportunity' Crim LR 245.

Rowbottom, J. (2006) 'Obscenity laws and the internet', Crim LR 97.

www.pearsoned.co.uk/lawexpress

 Go online to access more revision support including quizzes to test your knowledge, sample questions with answer guidelines, podcasts you can download, and more!

Terrorism

Revision checklist

Essentials points you should know:

☐ The definition of terrorism and the range of offences under the Terrorism Act 2000

☐ The stop and search powers given to the police under s 43 and the new section 47A of the Terrorism Act 2000

☐ Further offences under the Anti-terrorism, Crime and Security Act 2001. See especially the House of Lords' decision on Pt IV in *A*

☐ The repeal of the control order regime in the Prevention of Terrorism Act 2005 and the recent introduction of the Terrorism Prevention and Investigation of Measures Act 2011

Topic map

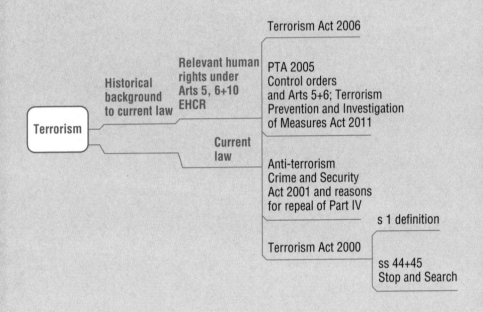

Terrorism

Historical background to current law

Relevant human rights under Arts 5, 6+10 EHCR

Current law

Terrorism Act 2006

PTA 2005
Control orders
and Arts 5+6; Terrorism
Prevention and Investigation
of Measures Act 2011

Anti-terrorism
Crime and Security
Act 2001 and reasons
for repeal of Part IV

Terrorism Act 2000

s 1 definition

ss 44+45
Stop and Search

A printable version of this topic map is available at www.pearsoned.co.uk/lawexpress

▉ Introduction

Anti-terrorism law is probably the fastest changing area of law addressed in any human rights course.

Major new legislation has gone through Parliament since 2000 and numerous key decisions have been made in the appellate courts which affect the interpretation of these new controls on terrorist suspects.

Few areas of law attract such public interest and it is not an exaggeration to state that in no other field has the Human Rights Act had such a significant impact on government policy.

ASSESSMENT ADVICE

It is very common for students to get carried away with terrorism law. The whole area is extremely controversial and it is likely that every single person you know has an opinion about terrorism and how it should be prevented. The key is to analyse the law dispassionately and logically, and not to try to impress the examiner with the strength of your feelings or, far worse, the depth of your understanding of the underlying politics. The best marks are achieved when, after setting out and discussing the law, the student displays greater understanding of the context, but it is absolutely crucial that you explain the law first.

Essay questions

These are likely to require you to consider the tensions between government policy and basic human rights, most obviously the rights to liberty, a fair trial, privacy and freedom of expression. Make sure you back up your arguments with examples of the ways in which government power to control terrorist activities is limited in the legislation and by judicial decision.

Problem questions

These are likely to be similar to police-powers problem questions: you will need to consider whether an offence has been made out and whether the police acted within the law. Again, make sure you back up your answer by reference to the latest relevant legislation and case law and make sure you read the question very carefully – examiners do not put in extra sentences for fun and every part of the scenario will be relevant. It is worth spending time reading the question, noting down the specific issues involved and the legislation engaged, as well as thoroughly planning your answer. The best answers are well structured and spot every issue in the question, and if you only read through the question very quickly, you are very likely to find that your answer misses a key issue which will lose you marks. Never forget to apply the law in detail to the particular issue under discussion.

Sample question

Could you answer this question? Below is a typical essay question that could arise on this topic. Guidelines on answering the question are included at the end of this chapter, whilst a sample problem question and guidance on tackling it can be found on the companion website.

ESSAY QUESTION

Present terrorism legislation provides the executive with too much power and is draconian, unjustifiable and wholly disproportionate to the situation existing today in the UK. Discuss.

Background

This chapter will examine the developments in anti-terrorism law since the Terrorism Act 2000, but you can be certain that by the time you are reading this book in print, a new case, a new policy or a new piece of legislation will be changing the law around terrorism once more. For example, you should particularly be aware of the repeal of the Prevention of Terrorism Act 2005, and the recent introduction of the Terrorism Prevention and Investigation of Measures Act 2011 ('TPIM').

The Terrorism Act 2000

The Terrorism Act 2000 (TA 2000) was designed to create a single legislative answer to the problems posed by terrorist activities. It creates a huge number of offences; it bans organisations and creates offences around being involved in those organisations, it deals with terrorist property, it grants a series of police powers but, firstly, it defines terrorism.

KEY STATUTE

Terrorism Act 2000, s 1

In general terms, terrorism means the use or threat of action which

■ causes some damage – against a person or property – or threatens to cause that damage,

- AND which is designed to influence the government or the general public,
- AND which is made to advance a political, religious or ideological cause.

Under section 40, a terrorist is anyone who commits an offence under the 2000 Act, or who is or has been involved in the commission, preparation or instigation of acts of terrorism.

 Make your answer stand out

It is crucial that you know and can apply section 1 because all of the offences in the TA 2000 are founded on this key definition. Defining terrorism is problematic, and the breadth and imprecision of the definition in s 1 TA 2000 has created a great deal of academic and political criticism. See 'Read to impress' at the conclusion of this chapter.

Under s 3(4) TA 2000, where the Secretary of State believes an organisation is concerned with terrorism – i.e., activities which fall into s 1 – he has the power to order that it be listed in Schedule 2 to the Act. Organisations listed in this Schedule are described as proscribed, and involvement in these organisations can result in a number of potential offences, set out in sections 11 to 13. See *Alton and others* v *Secretary of State for the Home Department* (2008) where the Court of Appeal decided that to proscribe an organisation now for what it may do in the future was too remote.

It is important to understand who bears the burden of in terrorist cases. For example, as regards s 11(2)(a) and (b) it is a defence for a person to prove (evidential burden) that when he was a member, the organisation had not been proscribed at that time, and, even if it was proscribed, he was not involved in the activities of that organisation during that period (see below the case of *Attorney-General's Reference (No. 4 of 2002)* (2003)).

KEY CASE

Attorney-General's Reference (No. 4 of 2002) [2003] 3 WLR 976

Concerning: burden of proof under section 11 of the TA 2000

Facts

The defendant was charged under s 11(1) of the TA 2000 for belonging to and professing to belong to a proscribed organisation ('Hamas'). After the judge ruled that there was no case to answer, the Attorney-General referred the matter to the Court of Appeal for their opinion

▶

on, *inter alia,* whether s 11(2) imposed an evidential or legal burden on the accused. The Court of Appeal opined that s 11(2) demanded a legal burden of proof. The matter was then referred (on application by the defendant's counsel) to the House of Lords.

Legal principle

Lord Bingham considered a number of factors including the following;

(1) The presumption of innocence – his Lordship stated that there could be a real risk of an unfair

(2) Conviction if defendants in this situation had to prove their defence on a balance of probabilities. There was a risk that if they failed to establish a defence, they might be convicted on the basis of conduct which was not criminal at the date of commission.

(3) The difficulties of proving the legal burden – it might well be impossible for the defendant to show that he had not taken part in the organisation's activities at any time whilst it was proscribed. After all, other members of the group were unlikely to testify on his behalf; such organisations do not keep minutes of their meetings nor have any records or documents that he could avail of for use in his defence. Even the defendant's own verbal testimony may be seen as suspect and unreliable.

(4) Accordingly, the majority of the House of Lords (Lord Rodger and Lord Carswell dissenting) decided in favour of imposing an evidential burden of proof only.

Most controversially, under s 13 offences include wearing an item of clothing or wearing, carrying or displaying an article in such a way as to arouse reasonable suspicion that the person is a member or a supporter of a proscribed organisation. 'Articles' has a very broad meaning and is not restricted to weapons and the like, but also extends to any document, record, disc, data, etc – indeed anything that could be used for a purpose connected with terrorist activities.

A key case in this area is *R* v *Zafar and Others* (2008).

KEY CASE

R v *Zafar and Others* [2008] EWCA Crim 184

Concerning: the mens rea of section 57 of the TA 2000

Facts

The appellants were found in possession of documents, including compact discs/ computer hard drives, ideological propaganda material, extremist literature, plans (the prosecution allege) to go to Pakistan to train and then to Afghanistan to fight. The question was whether there was a direct connection between the objects possessed and acts of terrorism. The prosecution argued that the defendants intended to use the articles as a means of inciting the others to commit acts of terrorism.

Legal principle

The court doubted whether there was a case of infringement of s 57 that could properly be left up to the jury. The judge's direction to the jury appeared to be unsatisfactory and inadequate. The judge should have directed the jury that 'they had to be satisfied that each appellant *intended to use the relevant articles to incite his fellow planners* to fight in Afghanistan'. This had not been done and, accordingly, their convictions were quashed. Hence, s 57 must now be read that an offence will be committed only 'if he possessed an article in circumstances which gave rise to a reasonable suspicion that he *intended* it to be used for the purpose of the commission, preparation or instigation of an act of terrorism'.

You should be aware that in order for s 57 to constitute an offence the *purpose* of possessing the material must be linked in some way to an act of terrorism. However, s 58(1) states that a person commits an offence if:

(a) he collects or makes a record of information of a kind likely to be useful to a person committing or preparing an act of terrorism, or
(b) he possesses a document or record containing information of that kind.

The emphasis of s 57 is placed on 'the purpose' of being in possession of the articles, i.e. for conduct relevant to terrorism, whilst s 58 concentrates on records or documents 'of a kind likely to be useful' to persons concerned with terrorism. See *R* v *Rowe* (2007); *R* v *G*; *R* v *J* (2009).

✎ EXAM TIP

A key point to observe about terrorism offences is their breadth. Many individuals would be open to arrest under the charge of possessing information likely to be useful to terrorists. The wide discretion over who to arrest is therefore left to the authorities, and this clearly conflicts with a key part of criminal and human rights law – that law should be certain and universally applicable.

Stop and search powers and terrorism

Under s 43 of the TA 2000 a constable must have *reasonable grounds of suspicion* for stopping and searching a person. Unlike s 1 of PACE, once the reasonable grounds are established he may search the person to discover whether he has in his possession *anything* which may constitute evidence that he is a terrorist (s 43(1)), and seize and retain anything found on that person (s 43(4)). However, sections 44–47 have now been repealed since in *Gillan and Quinton* v *UK* (2010) the European Court held, *inter alia*, that since the statutory provisions were not in accordance with the law there was a violation of Article 8. The remaining relevant sections are now section 43 and the new section 47A–47C (Terrorism Act (Remedial) Order 2011). See also the Code of Practice within Schedule 6B to the Terrorism Act 2000.

Replacement powers to stop and search in specified location

KEY STATUTE

The Terrorism Act 2000 (Remedial) Order 2011, s 47A

Under Section 47A(1) a senior police officer may give an authorisation under subsection (2) or (3) in relation to a specified area or place if the officer *reasonably suspects* that an act of terrorism will take place. Sections 47(2)–(5) authorises any constable in uniform to stop a vehicle in the specified area or place and to search a pedestrian or a vehicle; but only for the purpose of discovering whether there is anything which may constitute evidence that the vehicle concerned is being used for the purposes of terrorism. No reasonable grounds are necessary to suspect that such evidence exists.

As a result of this new section a senior police office, i.e. one of at least the rank of assistant chief constable, will be able to make the initial decision to order the stop and search of individuals or vehicles where he reasonably suspects acts of terrorism. However, he must then inform the Secretary of State within 48 hours, or the order will expire.

✎ EXAM TIP

You should take note that the ghost of the repealed s 44 still appears to be present in the guise of section 47A, since that section does not include the normal requirement for reasonable grounds of suspicion on the part of the constable prior to him making the actual stop and search (see s 47A(5)). So, in a problem question, keep in mind the previous law and cases relating to previous sections 44–47.

■ The Anti-terrorism, Crime and Security Act 2001

ATCSA was passed in the months following the attacks in America on 11 September. Its 14 Parts included new regulations to control terrorist property and created new police powers, including the power to remove disguises.

Part IV and detention of foreign nationals without trial

However, the most controversial part of the Act was the now repealed Part IV. Under sections 21 to 35, foreign nationals who were suspected of being involved with terrorism could be held indefinitely without being charged or tried for any offence. This was repealed as a consequence of the extremely important case of *A* v *Secretary of State for the Home Department* (2004).

A v *Secretary of State for the Home Department* [2004] UKHL 56

Concerning: Pt IV ATCSA and Articles 5, 14 and 15 of the ECHR

Facts

A was one of 14 individuals detained under Pt IV ATCSA who appealed to the House of Lords after the Court of Appeal had overturned a decision of the Special Immigration Appeal Commission (SIAC).

A's arguments were that

(1) the derogation under Article 15 from the right to liberty under Article 5 was impermissible because there was no public emergency threatening the life of the nation;

(2) the derogation was not proportionate because alternative means could achieve the same result; and

(3) that s 23 was discriminatory because it allowed for the detention without trial of foreign nationals but not UK citizens. (NB: there had been no derogation from Article 14: freedom from discrimination.)

Legal principle

On the first point the majority of the House (8 of 9 Law Lords) held that the decision as to whether there was a public emergency threatening the life of the nation was a pre-eminently political one and that the government and SIAC were entitled to conclude there had been such an emergency. The minority judgment of Lord Hoffman, however, was very strong on this point (he agreed with the majority on the second point) – arguing that there was no public emergency arising from terrorism, but rather that the life of the nation could be threatened by an overly restrictive reaction to terrorism which impinged on basic liberties.

On the second point, 8 of the 9 Law Lords (Lord Walker dissenting) held that the derogation was disproportionate because it did not deal with UK citizens who were potential terrorists, and it allowed those detained to leave the UK freely and carry out terrorist activities elsewhere. The measures were therefore not strictly required by the exigencies of the situation.

On the discrimination point, the majority (with Lord Walker dissenting again) held that the measure was discriminatory and could not be justified. Also, in breaching Article 26 ▶

of the International Covenant on Civil and Political Rights 1966, it was inconsistent with the UK's other international obligations in the definition of Article 15.

The result was that the 2001 designated derogation order was quashed and a declaration of incompatibility was made in relation to s 23 ATCSA 2001 as being incompatible with Article 5 and Article 14.

With the policy in tatters, the government then set about trying to control the activities of these suspected terrorists without breaching human rights law. The answer the Home Secretary found was 'control orders'.

📖 **REVISION NOTE**

The key rights discussed in *A* are Articles 14 and 15, outlined in Chapter 1 on the ECHR. Article 14 is discussed in more detail in the Discrimination chapter. Article 5 is clearly relevant but it was not at issue before the Law Lords. Knowing the content of these rights – for example, the conditions which permit a state to derogate under Article 15 – is the foundation for understanding and explaining why the House of Lords found that the derogation was impermissible and s 23 was incompatible with Articles 5 and 14.

■ The Prevention of Terrorism Act 2005

With the Prevention of Terrorism Act 2005 (PTA), the government took the idea of civil orders to control the activity of individuals from antisocial behaviour law into anti-terrorism law. These became known as 'control orders'. Control orders created a legal structure under which the lives and activity of suspected terrorists could be restricted and controlled, without having to prosecute or, in some cases, being unable to deport such individuals. It was also an attempt to increase judicial oversight and involvement in the process in order to try to avoid the possibility of the courts making another ruling like *A*. The spirit of *A* v *Secretary of State for the Home Department* appears to have been finally laid to rest by the decision of *A and Others* v *United Kingdom* (2009).

KEY CASE

A and Others v *UK* (2009) 49 EHRR 625

Concerning: Articles 3, 5, 14 and 15 of the ECHR

Facts

After the decision of the House of Lords, the applicants complained of a number of Convention violations, including Articles 3, 5 (and specifically 5(1)(f) and 5(4)), 14 and 15).

Legal principle

In relation to Article 3, the court stated that even though the applicants' detention may have caused anxiety and distress, that fear was alleviated by the prospect that they were entitled to challenge the legality of the detention via the courts. Indeed, they had already done so successfully in the House of Lords. Accordingly, the court found that there had not been a violation of Article 3.

As regards Article 5(1) and in particular 5(1)(f), i.e. detaining a person with a view to deportation or extradition, the court observed that the domestic laws in relation to keeping 'under active review' the question as to whether or not to deport a detainee were not 'sufficiently certain or determinative', and therefore amounted to a violation of Article 5(1)(f).

Further, in the absence of a valid derogation, indefinite detention was a violation of Article 5(1). However, the applicants argued that there was no public emergency threatening the life of a nation as set out in Article 15 for the following reasons: 'first, the emergency was neither actual nor imminent; secondly, it was not of a temporary nature; and, thirdly, the practice of other States, none of which had derogated from the Convention, together with the informed views of other national and international bodies, suggested that the existence of a public emergency had not been established'. The court held (in agreeing with the majority of the House of Lords) that there had been a public emergency threatening the life of the nation.

Finally, the court also agreed with the House of Lords in their findings that discriminating between nationals and non-nationals was contrary to Article 14 and accordingly was a violation of Article 5(1).

! Don't be tempted to . . .

Narrow revision is very dangerous. It is crucial here to understand Articles 3, 5 and 6 discussed in Chapter 1 on the ECHR. What rights do these Articles contain and when will the rights in them be engaged?

Control orders

Whilst 'control orders' have now been repealed, the practice of restrictions to individuals remains intact under the recently introduced statute, The Terrorism Prevention and Investigation Measures Act 2011. Gone is the identifying name 'control orders', replaced by 'TPIM notice'. The new Act has been described as merely a watering-down of control orders. Hence, in order to understand the new system, and how future court decisions may interpret TPIMs, it is essential to understand the prior law.

Prevention of Terrorism Act 2005, s 1

Under s 1 PTA 2005, the Secretary of State or the courts have the power to impose an order 'against an individual that imposes obligations on him for purposes connected with protecting members of the public from a risk of terrorism'.

The only obligations which can be imposed are those obligations the Secretary of State or the court consider necessary 'for purposes connected with preventing or restricting involvement by that individual in terrorism-related activity' (s 1(3) PTA 2005).

In October 2007, the House of Lords delivered judgments on the legitimacy of the control order regime in three linked cases which are discussed below.

KEY CASE

Secretary of State for the Home Department v *JJ and Others* [2007] UKHL 45

Concerning: non-derogating control orders and the right to liberty in Article 5 ECHR

Facts

In JJ the Secretary of State imposed non-derogating control orders on six foreign nationals with a large number of restrictions on their freedom. The government argued that these measures restricted movement but did not contravene Article 5 and that, if they did deprive JJ of the right to liberty, the correct action by the judge would be to amend the control order, not quash it.

Legal principle

The majority (4 of 5) held that, following EctHR rulings, the test of whether a measure deprived an individual of their right to liberty involved considering all of the factors including the nature, duration, effects, and manner of implementation of the measure. Taking all of the factors into account, the majority felt that the original decision to quash the orders was not wrong in law.

KEY CASE

Secretary of State for the Home Department v *MB and AF* [2007] UKHL 46

Concerning: non-derogating control orders and the right to a fair trial

Facts

In *MB/AF*, the applicants were again subject to non-derogating control orders, but in this case the House of Lords had to consider the control order regime and the right to a fair trial under Article 6. The key questions the Law Lords had to consider were:

(1) whether non-derogating control orders constituted a criminal charge under Article 6 ECHR;

(2) whether the procedure to make a control order was compatible with Article 6 when the person accused had no chance to defend the charges against them because the allegations were all restricted and the case was defended by special advocates; and

(3) if the procedures were not compatible could they be read down using s 3 HRA 1998 so as to become Convention-compliant?

Legal principle

The Law Lords held that (i) whilst control orders are restrictive of liberty, they are essentially preventative, and are not designed to be punitive or retributive. Also, there is no identification of a specific criminal offence or an assertion of criminal conduct; there is only a foundation of suspicion. In response to question (ii), they held that the special advocate procedure was likely to protect most individuals from injustice and therefore met the requirements of Article 6, but it could not be guaranteed to do so – in some cases, the procedure would be incompatible with Article 6. However, each case must be considered on its merits.

In relation to (iii) the majority (3 of 5) held that the procedures could be made Convention-compliant using s 3 HRA. Where there was restricted material, the court has to decide whether allowing that information to remain closed to the defendant would be incompatible with their right to a fair trial. If it would, and the Secretary of State still refuses to reveal it to the defendant, the court can rule that the information is inadmissible or is not to be relied upon. If the information is crucial to the government's case, then removing it will make the decision flawed and the order will have to be quashed. In this way, the procedure can be made to be compliant with Article 6.

See also *Secretary of State for the Home Department* v *AM* [2009] EWHC 572 (Admin), where the appellant lost his appeal against the curfew terms of his control order being extended from 8 to 12 hours per day (with limited exceptions).

The final case in this trio was *Secretary of State for the Home Department* v *E and Another* (2007) which concerned the question of whether or not it was vital to consider a prosecution before making a control order. The House of Lords held it was fundamental to the control order regime that, where a prosecution was possible, individuals should be prosecuted rather than being made subject to control orders. However, failing to consider a prosecution or consult a senior officer will not automatically make the decision to make a control order flawed, but it would strongly support an argument by the defendant that the decision was flawed.

Lawfulness of control order based on 'closed material'

Any appeal by a controlee against the implementation of a control order invariably involved matters of national security. As a result, unlike a normal appeal, the appellant may not be entitled to review all, if any, of the evidence against him. Certain evidence, known as 'closed material' may be withheld for numerous reasons, including matters relating to the intelligent services and their sources, e.g. their personnel, informants and well as other information-gathering techniques; these may all be jeopardised, if disclosed. However, the appellant is entitled to a fair hearing, and part of that process is the entitlement that the appellant be aware of material that is ultimately being used to deprive him of his liberty. Thus the procedural protection afforded to an individual must include at least sufficient informational details of the allegations made against him, in order to be able to provide his special advocate with proper instructions to contest the case; otherwise it cannot be said that he received a fair hearing.

KEY CASE

A and Others v UK (2009) 49 EHRR 625

Concerning: violation of Article 5(4)

Facts

The applicants complained before the Grand Chamber that, *inter alia*, there had been a breach of Article 5(4), i.e. proceedings to determine the lawfulness of their detention in that, as a result of the 'closed material' not being made available to them, they were not only prevented from assessing the lawfulness of their detention but were also unable to properly respond to the accusations made against them. The question thus arose was whether due to the absence of the closed material the applicants were deprived of a fair trial.

Legal principle

The court stated that the detainees must be provided with *sufficient* information about the allegations against them to enable them to give *effective* instructions to their counsel (in this instance, a special advocate) to properly defend themselves.

 Make your answer stand out

Good answers may point out that the strict rule emanating from *A and Others* v *UK* is that where the detention was based solely or to a decisive degree on closed material the procedural requirements of Article 5(4) would not be satisfied. This decision came a week before the domestic case of *Secretary of State for the Home Department* v *AF, AN and AE* (2009) where control orders were made against the appellants and based predominantly or wholly upon closed material. Somewhat reluctantly their Lordships and Ladyship abided by the judgment in *A* and the appeals in that case were allowed.

■ The Terrorism Prevention and Investigation Measures Act 2011 (TPIMA)

On the 15 December 2011, as a result of the controversial, unsatisfactory (and many would argue, draconian) restrictions placed on individuals via control orders, the government set about introducing a similar version, known as the 'TPIM notice'. As with all anti-terrorism legislation, the primary purpose of such measures is to protect the public.

Like their predecessor, TPIMs are supposedly to be preventative in nature and practice and are seen as an alternative and final response to dealing with terrorist suspects where there is insufficient evidence or any realistic prospects of a successful prosecution.

KEY STATUTE

The Terrorism Prevention and Investigation Measures Act 2011

In s 2(1) The Secretary of State may by notice (a 'TPIM notice') impose specified terrorism prevention and investigation measures on an individual if conditions A to E in section 3 are met. Section 3(1) Condition A is that the Secretary of State reasonably believes that the individual is, or has been, involved in terrorism-related activity; s 3(2) Condition B is that some or all of the relevant activity is new terrorism-related activity; s 3(3) and (4) are Conditions C and D and state that where the Secretary of State reasonably considers that it is necessary, for purposes connected with protecting members of the public from a risk of terrorism, or preventing or restricting the individual's involvement in terrorism-related activity, for terrorism prevention and investigation measures to be imposed on the individual.

Like the now defunct control orders, where there is insufficient evidence to prosecute individuals for terrorism-related activities, or where the state is unable to deport such persons, a TPIM notice may now be issued against them. The period for any TPIM notice is one year, but may be extended to a maximum of two years, provided conditions A C and D are complied with (see section 5). In total, the TPIMA consists of 31 sections and 8 Schedules. Schedule 1 deals primarily with the measures that may be imposed by the Secretary of State under a TPIM notice against the particular individual(s), and you should be familiar with them.

The remainder of the schedules include such matters as urgent cases that require immediate TPIM action, without the need for first obtaining permission by the court under section 6 (see Schedule 2); appeals against convictions (Sch. 3); proceedings relating to TPIMs (Sch. 4); powers of entry, search, seizure and retention (Sch. 5); fingerprints and samples (Sch. 6).

✎ EXAM TIP

At the time of writing, no cases have yet been decided under this Act. Should an exam question arise in the area of TPIMs, you will invariably need to consider and compare the old with the new. The new legislation is meant to include significant modifications and apparently overcome the many deficiencies of the now abandoned control orders. Also, the imposition of a TPIM notice is meant to be less intrusive, prohibitive and restrictive. Whether the resulting legislation has actually achieved this is very debatable. Even at this early stage there have been suggestions that the Act is merely a diluted version of control orders, and that any type of future legal action against such notices is likely to encounter similar legal arguments as its predecessor.

  Make your answer stand out

When discussing this area of law you should point out possible violations of Articles 5, 6 and 8 of the ECHR.

▉ Terrorism Act 2006

The London bombings of 7 July 2005 were the catalyst for the introduction of the Terrorism Act 2006 (TA 2006). The Act not only creates new offences but also amends existing anti-terrorist legislation and deals with the lacunae from previous legislation. The Terrorism Act 2006 makes some amendments to the TA 2000, including increasing the period of pre-charge detention from 7 to 28 days (although at the time of writing the Protection of Freedoms Bill is going through Parliament and it is expected that the 28 days be reduced to 14 days), and creates some new offences, including preparation of terrorist acts, providing or receiving training for terrorism-related purposes or encouraging terrorism.

KEY STATUTE

Terrorism Act 2006, s 1

Under section 1(1) the particular statement must be 'likely' to be interpreted by those who receive it as an encouragement to commence some terrorist conduct. Whether or not this is so is to be determined by considering (a) 'the contents of the statement as a whole; and(b) to the circumstances and manner of its publication.' (see s 1(4)(a) and (b)). In *R* v *Abdul Rahman and Bilal Mohammed* (2008) the court stated that in relation to intention or recklessness, when assessing culpability, the 'volume and content of the material disseminated will be relevant to the harm caused, intended or foreseeable.

Sections 5, 6 and 8 specifically deal with the preparation and training for terrorism. These provisions include offences related to the instruction and training of persons for various skills in the deployment of dangerous materials and/or substances for the purposes of terrorism. Indeed, even being at a place where such instruction or training is occurring or which involves weapon training, as in section 54(1) of the TA 2000, may constitute an offence, provided the person knew or was aware that the training was connected with the commission or preparation of a terrorist act.

KEY CASE

R v *Da Costa; R* v *Ahmet; R* v *Hamid; R* v *Ahmed;*
R v *Al-Figari* [2009] EWCA Crim 482

Concerning: ss 5, 6 and 8 of the Terrorism Act 2006

Facts

The applicants C, AA, H, AK and AF attended various meetings and training camps in the New Forest and Berkshire, mostly organised by H. As a result of what had occurred at these meetings H and C were convicted under section 6 of providing training or instruction for terrorism purposes. AK and AF were found guilty of offences under section 8 of attending such training camps (AA was convicted of soliciting to murder, along with H). Thereafter the applicants applied for leave to appeal against their convictions.

Legal principle

The main questions in issue concerned the directions given by the trial judge to the jury. It appeared that the jury may have been confused regarding the requirements of and differences between section 6(1)(b), i.e. intending to use the acquired skills for terrorism purposes, and section 8, where no such intention is required. Thus, under section 8 the offence may still be committed even in the absence of possessing the intention of using his training for terrorist activities, provided he knows or realises that his teaching and training were for the purposes of terrorism and that they were in fact being given for those purposes. The court found that the trial judge's direction to the jury on this point was correct and accordingly, for this and other reasons, refused their applications for leave to appeal.

The remaining sections under Part 1 of the Act deal mainly with very serious terrorist offences involving making and possessing various devices and materials, such as using radioactive matter against nuclear sites (section 9); the misuse of such materials and the damage of facilities (section 10); terrorists threats (section 11); and trespassing on to nuclear sites (section 12).

✎ EXAM TIP

The vagueness of many of the definitions in the TA 2006 have been subject to a great deal of academic criticism and any exam question which requires consideration of terrorism offences and human rights would not be complete without an explanation of this latest law and the relationship with freedom of expression as guaranteed by Article 10 ECHR (see, for example, the discussion by Adrian Hunt in the June 2007 edition of Criminal Law Review, pp 441–58).

■Putting it all together

Answer guidelines

See the essay question at the start of the chapter.

Approaching the question

This question needs a detailed, relevant and up-to-date application of terrorism law.

Important points to include

- Introduction: define the elements of the question; what is the legislation, what offences and controls do the Acts contain? Define and discuss the definition of 'terrorism' in s 1 TA 2000. Explain how you will examine the breadth of the power given to the executive, and limitations on that power contained in (1) the legislation itself and (2) judicial decisions based on ECHR rights.

- Consider elements of the legislation: for example, compare the present and previous powers to stop and search under ss 43, 44 and 45 under TA 2000 with the newly introduced section 47A.

- Examine whether or not The Terrorism Prevention and Investigation of Measures Act 2011 (TPIM) is merely 'control orders' under a different name.

- Explain the powers and the limits on these powers contained in the legislation. Consider judicial decisions in relation to these powers and other anti-terrorism laws: have the judiciary decided that all current terrorism law is unjustifiable? When have they decided it is justifiable – e.g. *Gillan* v *UK* (2010), *E* v Secretary of State for the Home Department (2009) – and why? When have they decided that it is unjustifiable – e.g. *A* v Secretary of State for the Home Department (2004), *JJ* v Secretary of State for the Home Department (2007), *MB* v Secretary of State for the Home Department (2006) – and why have they decided this?

- Conclusion: draw these threads together; do you consider that the law is disproportionate?

Make your answer stand out

As we stated above, the classic mistake to make in answering terrorism questions is to believe the examiner wants to hear your opinions on why the laws are too weak or too draconian, without explaining the laws themselves and discussing judicial decisions on the legislation. Virtually all of your colleagues will probably answer the terrorism question on the exam, and the way to make your answer stand out is to get these basics right, and then to know the background to the legislation, be confident with all sides of the argument on a particular issue, and to be able to tie your answer in to the underlying philosophical and legal human rights issues.

READ TO IMPRESS

Hunt, A. (2007) '*Criminal prohibitions on direct and indirect encouragement of terrorism*', Crim LR, Jun, 441–58.

Middleton, B. (2007) '*Control orders: out of control*', Crim LR 173, 3–5.

Walker, C. (2007) 'The legal definition of "Terrorism" in United Kingdom law and beyond', *Public Law*, Summer, 331–52.

Walker, C. (2008) '*Terrorism: Terrorism Act 2000, ss 1 and 58 – possession of terrorist documents*', Crim LR 2, 160–5.

www.pearsoned.co.uk/lawexpress

 Go online to access more revision support including quizzes to test your knowledge, sample questions with answer guidelines, podcasts you can download, and more!

Discrimination

9

Revision checklist

Essential points you should know:

- [ ] Prohibited grounds of discrimination under the Equality Act 2010
- [ ] The changes introduced by the Equality Act 2010
- [ ] The significance of the HRA and the ECHR in this context, particularly the relevance of Art. 14
- [ ] Any other international approaches to discrimination relevant to your syllabus, and the history of UK discrimination legislation if that is relevant to your syllabus

■Topic map

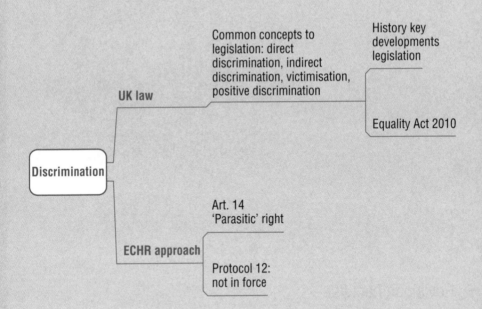

Discrimination

UK law

Common concepts to legislation: direct discrimination, indirect discrimination, victimisation, positive discrimination

History key developments legislation

Equality Act 2010

ECHR approach

Art. 14 'Parasitic' right

Protocol 12: not in force

A printable version of this map is available from **www.pearsoned.co.uk/lawexpress**

■ Introduction

Some forms of discrimination are lawful and even justifiable.

The law on murder discriminates against people who kill with the requisite *mens rea*, but this does not mean that it is inappropriate. The law on discrimination attempts to deal with unjustifiable discrimination.

Discrimination is a very broad field. It requires knowledge of domestic and international approaches to a range of forms of discrimination. You will need to know the main details of the domestic legislation dealing with discrimination, as well as the way that the ECHR deals with discrimination. You will also need to be familiar with the arguments for and against these laws as they have been interpreted by the domestic courts and the ECtHR, as well as proposals for reform in this area.

■ Background

This area of the law is extremely complicated, even after the consolidation and clarification under the Equality Act 2010. Before that Act, the principal domestic legislation consisted of the Equal Pay Act 1970, the Sex Discrimination Act 1975, the Race Relations Act 1976, the Disability Discrimination Act 1995, the Gender Recognition Act 2005, the Civil Partnership Act 2005, the Employment Equality (Age) Regulations 2006 and the Equality Act 2006. Between them, these pieces of legislation dealt with discrimination on the grounds of sex, race, disability, sexual orientation, age and religion. The legislation shared common concepts, such as direct and indirect discrimination, but there were differences between the various anti-discrimination regimes: for example, in the scope of the coverage of the schemes. The Equality Act 2010 is to be welcomed for resolving many of the differences and difficulties, but it is still open to criticism for not going far enough. The source of much of the intricacy in this area is the relationship between domestic law, ECtHR cases and EU legislation. For a complete picture, you must consider domestic law in conjunction with the EU law that it is designed to implement in this country. Make sure that you know whether the relevant EU provisions are on your syllabus! In addition, you must be familiar with the significance of the ECHR in general and Article 14 of the ECHR in particular. Article 14 deals with discrimination 'on any ground', and therefore extends to discrimination not generally regulated by English or EU law. However, it is limited to discrimination regarding the rights and freedoms provided elsewhere in the Convention and this proved to be a significant limitation on its use and effectiveness.

ASSESSMENT ADVICE

Essays questions tend to predominate in this area. Everyone accepts that certain discrimination is inappropriate, but there is a disagreement on what amounts to unjustifiable discrimination, how the law should deal with it, and whether the law is

▶

in fact the best instrument to tackle it. You must display a sound understanding of the main domestic legislation, Art. 14 of the ECHR, and relevant domestic and ECtHR cases. Essay questions frequently require you to assess the validity of Art. 14 and the various domestic laws on discrimination. These questions require you to critically analyse relevant legislation and case law and consider whether they are effective in protecting individuals from unjustifiable discrimination. Essay questions may also ask you whether discrimination laws 'go too far' and prohibit behaviour that should be lawful or have an unintended adverse consequence on the group that they are meant to protect. You must consider carefully the arguments for and against the laws in question and any reform proposals. You need to consider the purpose of the laws and the distinctions between them, and to back up your arguments with reference to relevant case law and particular statutory provisions as well as academic and other commentary.

■ Sample question

Could you answer this question? Below is a typical essay question that could arise on this topic. Guidelines on answering the question are included at the end of this chapter, whilst a sample problem question and guidance on tackling it can be found on the companion website.

ESSAY QUESTION

'The domestic legislation and the ECHR do not go far enough to prohibit discrimination.'

Discuss.

📖 REVISION NOTE

You need to know the main domestic legislation and the way that the ECHR deals with discrimination. You should check your syllabus in order to determine whether you also need to know relevant EC legislation and case law. You should see the HRA chapter for the right to freedom from discrimination as it pertains to transsexuals.

■ Common concepts

The domestic legislation prohibits **direct discrimination**, **indirect discrimination**, and **victimisation** on the specified grounds. We will concentrate on the Equality Act 2010 but since it is new legislation and it will be some time before there is a detailed body of case law interpreting it, we will also refer to cases decided under the Sex Discrimination Act 1975 and the Race Relations Act 1976 (which have now been repealed, but many of their provisions are codified in the new Act).

KEY DEFINITIONS: Protected characteristic:

The 2010 Act groups together the grounds of disability which existed under the prior statutes and calls them 'protected characteristics'. They are age, disability, gender reassignment, marriage/civil partnership, pregnancy/maternity, race, religion/belief, sex, sexual orientation. You should be familiar with the statutory definition of each, and how they have been interpreted in relevant cases.

Direct discrimination: the Equality Act 2010 has consolidated and amended the existing law here.

Section 13, Direct discrimination:

(1) A person (A) discriminates against another (B) if, because of a protected characteristic, A treats B less favourably than A treats or would treat others.

(2) If the protected characteristic is age, A does not discriminate against B if A can show A's treatment of B to be a proportionate means of achieving a legitimate aim.

(3) If the protected characteristic is disability, and B is not a disabled person, A does not discriminate against B only because A treats or would treat disabled persons more favourably than A treats B.

(4) If the protected characteristic is marriage and civil partnership, this section applies to a contravention of Part 5 (work) only if the treatment is because it is B who is married or a civil partner.

(5) If the protected characteristic is race, less favourable treatment includes segregating B from others.

(6) If the protected characteristic is sex –

   (a) less favourable treatment of a woman includes less favourable treatment of her because she is breast-feeding;
   (b) in a case where B is a man, no account is to be taken of special treatment afforded to a woman in connection with pregnancy or childbirth.

'Direct' discrimination consists of less favourable treatment on prohibited grounds. The law employs a 'but for' test here. As Lord Goff put it in *James* v *Eastleigh BC* (1990), 'cases of direct [sex] discrimination … can be considered by asking the simple question: would the complainant have received the same treatment from the defendant but for his or her sex?'

However, since direct discrimination occurs where the complainant is treated less favourably than another person would be, if there were no other material difference in their circumstances than the protected characteristic (s 23 Equality Act 2010), There has been particular difficulty in some cases in finding the appropriate 'comparator', as in the case of *Eweida* v *British Airways* (2010).

►

Case	Decision
Rutherford v *Secretary of State for Trade and Industry* (2006)	The ratio of men and women who were adversely affected by a particular provision was 1:1.4. This was insufficient to establish the necessary degree of disparate impact as between men and women. This case concerned an equal pay claim under Art. 14 of the European Convention, but it has clear implications for all domestic law on indirect discrimination.
Coker v *Lord Chancellor* (2001)	A condition or requirement excluding almost the entire pool of potential candidates for an appointment could not constitute indirect discrimination.
Hampson v *Department of Education and Science* (1990)	The reasonable needs of the party who applies a condition should be balanced against the discriminatory effect of the condition in considering whether it is 'justifiable' for the purposes of s 1(1)(b)(ii) of the Race Relations Act 1976.
GMB v *Allen* (2008)	There is no indirect discrimination if the defendant seeks to achieve legitimate aims by proportionate means, but a defendant does not have a 'margin of discretion' in this respect.
R (on the application of *E*) v *Governing Body of JFS and Others (2009)*	Baroness Hale said: 'The basic difference between direct and indirect discrimination is plain ... The rule against direct discrimination aims to achieve formal equality of treatment: there must be no less favourable treatment between otherwise similarly situated people on [prohibited grounds]. Indirect discrimination looks beyond formal equality towards a more substantive equality of results: criteria which appear neutral on their face may have a disproportionately adverse impact upon people [with a particular protected characteristic]. Direct and indirect discrimination are mutually exclusive. You cannot have both at once ... The main difference between them is that direct discrimination cannot be justified. Indirect discrimination can be justified if it is a proportionate means of achieving a legitimate aim.'

Indirect discrimination: 'Indirect' discrimination concerns requirements, conditions, provisions, criteria, or practices that are apparently neutral but which have a significantly disproportionate and unjustifiable adverse effect on members of a particular group. Again, the 2010 Act has consolidated the law here.

Section 19 Indirect discrimination:

(1)   A person (A) discriminates against another (B) if A applies to B a provision, criterion or practice which is discriminatory in relation to a relevant protected characteristic of B's.

(2)   For the purposes of subsection (1), a provision, criterion or practice is discriminatory in relation to a relevant protected characteristic of B's if –

(a)   A applies, or would apply, it to persons with whom B does not share the characteristic,

(b)   it puts, or would put, persons with whom B shares the characteristic at a particular disadvantage when compared with persons with whom B does not share it,

(c)   it puts, or would put, B at that disadvantage, and

(d)   A cannot show it to be a proportionate means of achieving a legitimate aim.

(3)   The relevant protected characteristics are –

age;

disability;

gender reassignment;

marriage and civil partnership;

race;

religion or belief;

sex;

sexual orientation.

Note that before the Equality Act 2010 indirect disability discrimination was not prohibited by a statutory provision.

Victimisation: 'Victimisation' for complaining about discrimination in good faith is itself a form of discrimination. The legislation on discrimination contains specific provisions which protect those who complain about discrimination in good faith, as well as various other people: for example, those who provide evidence or information in good faith in connection with proceedings brought against an alleged discriminator. See s 27 of the Equality Act 2010.

✎ EXAM TIP

Some of the changes in wording introduced by the 2010 Act may be significant, and others are just simplifications. For example, direct discrimination is now less favourable treatment *because of* a protected characteristic, rather than *on grounds of* such a characteristic. Is this significant or a simplification?

! Don't be tempted to . . .

The Equality Act 2010 is not yet fully in force, and some of its provisions may never be. Make sure that a provision is in force before you apply it, and be aware of why some provisions are controversial and not yet in force.

KEY CASE

Mandla v *Dowell Lee* [1983] 2 AC 548

Concerning: indirect racial discrimination

Facts

The two claimants, father and son, were Sikhs and wore turbans over their unshorn hair in accordance with their tenets. The headmaster of a school refused to admit the son as a pupil at the school because the claimants would not comply with the school uniform rules and agree to the son cutting his hair and ceasing to wear a turban. They alleged indirect racial discrimination.

Legal principle

The House of Lords held that the claimants had been the victims of racial discrimination. One of the main issues in this case was whether Sikhs are a racial group for the purposes of the 1976 Act, which turned on the definition of 'ethnic origins'. There were two substantive judgments. Lord Fraser held that an ethnic group for the purposes of the 1976 Act is one that regards itself, and is regarded by others, 'as a distinct community by virtue of certain characteristics'. He outlined two essential conditions in this respect: (1) 'a long shared history', which the group knows distinguishes it from other groups, 'and the memory of which it keeps alive'; and (2) 'a cultural tradition of its own'. He also identified five subsidiary factors, including matters such as 'a common geographical origin, or descent from a small number of common ancestors'. Lord Templeman agreed with Lord Fraser's conclusion about Sikhs, but more simply stated that the concept of 'ethnic origins' applies to groups that possess certain characteristics of a race, 'namely group descent, a group of geographical origin and a group history'.

Exam questions in this area might ask you about positive discrimination. You can impro
your exam performance in this respect by pointing out that the Equality Act 2010 allows
employers, service providers and other organisations to take positive action to enable
existing or potential employees or customers to overcome or minimise a disadvantage
arising from a protected characteristic.

Racial discrimination: some key cases under the 'old' law

Case	Decision
Commission for Racial Equality v *Dutton* (1989)	'Gypsies' in the narrow sense of that term are a racial group because they share certain important characteristics, such as a long common history, a common geographical origin, and certain customs.
Crown Suppliers (PSA) v *Dawkins* (1993)	Rastafarians are a religious sect and not an ethnic group, and their 60-year history was insufficient to amount to a 'long-shared history'.
Zarcynyska v *Levy* (1979)	A white employee who was dismissed for refusing to obey an employer's instructions not to serve black customers had been discriminated against on 'racial grounds', since to conclude otherwise would be to produce an injustice.
Redfearn v *Serco* (2006)	An employee who was dismissed because of his association with a political party known for its racially discriminatory policies was not dismissed 'on racial grounds'.

London Borough of Lewisham v *Malcolm* [2008] UKHL 43

Concerning: the appropriate comparator in disability discrimination and whether lack of knowledge of the disability is relevant

Facts

A tenant breached a tenancy agreement with his local authority by sub-letting the premises, and the local authority consequently sought a possession order. The local authority was unaware that the tenant suffered from schizophrenia. The tenant argued that he was a disabled person for the purposes of the 1995 Act. He claimed that the court could not make a possession order against him, since the possession proceedings were a form of

▶

unlawful discrimination contrary to ss 22(3)(c) and 24 of the 1995 Act. Section 22(3)(c) makes it unlawful for a person managing any premises 'to discriminate against a disabled person occupying those premises … by evicting the disabled person, or subjecting him to any other detriment'. Section 24 defines 'discrimination' for the purposes of s 22.

Legal principle

The House of Lords decided that the local authority was entitled to possession. It held that the tenant was a disabled person for the purposes of the Act, but that there had been no discrimination against him. According to the House, the proper comparator was a person without a mental disability who had sub-let the landlord's premises in breach of his tenancy agreement and gone to live elsewhere, i.e. acted in the same manner as the tenant. Since the local authority would have sought possession against any non-disabled tenant who had acted in this manner, the House held that the disabled tenant had not been treated less favourably than the comparator and therefore had not been discriminated against for the purposes of the Act. Knowledge of the disability by the alleged discriminator was a crucial factor, at least where the act was not 'inherently discriminatory'; for instance, Lord Bingham stated that 'knowledge, or at least imputed knowledge, is necessary', and Lord Scott similarly held that the tenant needed to show that his disability 'played some motivating part in the council's decision'.

! Don't be tempted to . . .

London Borough of Lewisham v *Malcolm* was a controversial decision, which led to change. You should realise that it overturned a long-standing Court of Appeal authority, *Clark* v *TDG Ltd* (1999) on the matter of the proper comparator. But you also need to understand that the Equality Act 2010 supersedes it, why this was done, and how. The effect of ss 15 and 19 of the Equality Act is that the decision in *Lewisham* v *Malcolm* has been reversed by statute.

KEY CASE

Eweida v *British Airways* [2010] EWCA Civ 80

Concerning: direct and indirect religious discrimination; the appropriate comparator

Facts

A Christian employee was asked to either not wear a cross around her neck or to cover it up. She refused, and claimed that the policy was discrimination on grounds of religion. The wearing of jewellery is required for some faiths but not for Christianity, and employees who were Sikh or Muslim were allowed to wear religious jewellery or garments. The tribunal found that the compulsory Sikh bracelet was not an appropriate comparison since the wearing of a visible cross is not required by Christianity. On appeal to the Court of Appeal, the issue was indirect discrimination.

Legal principle

The rule that personal jewellery should be concealed did not constitute indirect discrimination on grounds of religion or belief. The claimant suffered a disadvantage due to her personal beliefs, not as part of an identifiable section of the workforce who shared her beliefs. Her personal objection to the policy was not a requirement of her religion. Sedley LJ stated that even if the policy had constituted indirect discrimination, it would have been justified as a proportionate means of achieving a legitimate aim.

The Gender Recognition Act 2004

This provides transsexual people with legal recognition in their acquired gender.

The Civil Partnership Act 2004

Two people of the same sex cannot marry each other, but the Civil Partnership Act 2004 enables them to form a 'civil partnership'. Civil partners acquire the same or similar legal rights and responsibilities as married, opposite-sex couples.

✎ EXAM TIP

Civil partnerships are the same-sex equivalent of marriages. However, you should realise that there are differences between these two institutions, that there is important academic debate about whether these differences are appropriate, and that there is also academic debate about whether it is appropriate to have separate institutions at all. See the articles by McNorrie (2008) and Washington (2005).

The Equality Act 2006

Part 1 of this Act established the Commission for Equality and Human Rights (CEHR) and defines its duties and powers. The CEHR has the functions of the three previous equality commissions: the Equal Opportunities Commission, the Commission for Racial Equality, and the Disability Rights Commission, In addition, it has a duty to combat unlawful discrimination on the grounds of sexual orientation, religion or belief, and age, and a general responsibility to promote human rights. In this respect, 'human rights' means the rights under the ECHR, as well as 'other human rights' (s 9). Some of the other provisions of the 2006 Act have been superseded by the 2010 Act.

> ✎ **EXAM TIP**
>
> Exam questions often raise the role of the Equality and Human Rights Commission. It is therefore crucial that you understand its main powers and duties. You should consider its activities. Why did s 28 of the Equality Act 2006 give the Commission the power to provide legal assistance to individuals but not an obligation to assist in this respect? Is it appropriate for s 26 to grant the Commission exclusive standing to bring certain types of legal proceedings? Does the Commission have an important role in practice?

> ✓ Make your answer stand out
>
> Referring to the academic debate about the scope of discrimination law may improve your mark. Not all forms of unjustified discrimination are prohibited by domestic legislation. Why not? Should the domestic law cover any other forms of discrimination? See the article by Middlemiss (2007).

■ Changes introduced by the Equality Act 2010

It is very important that you understand what the purposes of the Act are, and the extent to which they have been achieved. Of course there will be further developments as cases interpret the provisions of the Act, but you also need to remember that some of it is not yet in force. According to the Explanatory Notes to the Act, it has the following key effects:

'The Act . . . :

■ places a new duty on certain public bodies to consider socio-economic disadvantage when making strategic decisions about how to exercise their functions [NB This duty is not in force and at the time of writing the government had no plans to bring it into force];

■ extends the circumstances in which a person is protected against discrimination, harassment or victimisation because of a protected characteristic;

■ extends the circumstances in which a person is protected against discrimination by allowing people to make a claim if they are directly discriminated against because of a combination of two relevant protected characteristics;

- creates a duty on listed public bodies when carrying out their functions and on other persons when carrying out public functions to have due regard when carrying out their functions to: the need to eliminate conduct which the Act prohibits; the need to advance equality of opportunity between persons who share a relevant protected characteristic and those who do not; and the need to foster good relations between people who share a relevant protected characteristic and people who do not. The practical effect is that listed public bodies will have to consider how their policies, programmes and service delivery will affect people with the protected characteristics;

- allows an employer or service provider or other organisation to take positive action so as to enable existing or potential employees or customers to overcome or minimise a disadvantage arising from a protected characteristic;

- extends the permission for political parties to use women-only shortlists for election candidates to 2030;

- enables an employment tribunal to make a recommendation to a respondent who has lost a discrimination claim to take certain steps to remedy matters not just for the benefit of the individual claimant (who may have already left the organisation concerned) but also the wider workforce;

- amends family property law to remove discriminatory provisions and provides additional statutory property rights for civil partners in England and Wales;

- amends the Civil Partnership Act 2004 to remove the prohibition on civil partnerships being registered in religious premises.

✓ Make your answer stand out

Given that some of the changes under the 2010 Act which were stated in its Explanatory Notes to be improvements in the law are not yet in force, such as the socio-economic disadvantage provision, good answers may consider whether this undermines the extent to which the Act achieves its aims.

The ECHR and the HRA

Article 14 of the ECHR prohibits discrimination in the protection of Convention rights, but you should remember that other Articles can be used to combat discrimination by themselves. See the relevant discussion in Chapters 1 and 2.

The ECHR, Art. 14

Article 14 does not provide a free-standing right to freedom from discrimination – see Chapter 2.

Burden v *UK* [2007] 1 FCR 69

Concerning: Art.1 of Protocol No. 1 and Art. 14

Facts

The applicants were unmarried sisters who had each made a will leaving all their property to the other. Domestic law would require them to pay inheritance tax on any assets received under the will when one of them died. Property which passes from one spouse or civil partner to another is exempt from inheritance tax, but the applicants were not entitled to marry or to form a civil partnership with each other. The applicants alleged that the UK had violated their rights under Art. 1 of Protocol No. 1 in conjunction with Art. 14.

Legal principle

Attaching special importance to the institutions of marriage and civil partnerships, the ECtHR concluded that the UK had not violated the ECHR. The complaint fell within the scope of Art. 1 of Protocol No. 1, which meant that Art. 14 was relevant. However, the ECtHR held that cohabiting sisters are materially different from a married or Civil-Partnership-Act couple, and that it followed that there had been no discrimination and hence no violation of the ECHR. As the court put it, this was not a case of a 'difference in the treatment of persons in relevantly similar situations'. Siblings may have a close relationship, but they have not made 'a public undertaking, carrying with it a body of rights and obligations of a contractual nature'.

Abdulaziz, Cabales and Balkandali v *UK* (1985) 7 EHRR 471

Concerning: Arts 3, 8 and 14

Facts

The applicants were lawfully and permanently resident in the UK. The application of immigration rules prevented their husbands from joining or remaining with them in the UK. These rules made it easier for a husband settled in the UK to obtain permission for his non-national spouse to enter or remain in the UK than for a wife in the equivalent circumstances to obtain the equivalent permission. The applicants all claimed that they had been victims of discrimination on grounds of sex and race, and that the UK had violated Arts 3, 8 and 14 of the Convention by reason of this discrimination.

Legal principle

The ECtHR held that the UK had violated Art. 8 in conjunction with Art. 14 by reason of sex discrimination, and that the absence of an effective remedy for this violation meant that the UK had also violated Art. 13. However, it held that there had been no breach of Art. 3. The ECtHR accepted that the immigration rules pursued a legitimate aim, namely the protection of the UK labour market. Nonetheless, it held that this did not justify the difference in treatment between men and women. The court found that there had been no discrimination on the grounds of race because the relevant immigration rules 'did not contain regulations differentiating ... on the ground of ... race or ethnic origin', and that there had been no violation of Art. 3 because the difference in treatment 'was not designed to, and did not, humiliate or debase' the applicants.

KEY CASE

Pretty v UK (2002) 35 EHRR 1

Concerning: Arts 2, 3, 8, 9 and 14

Facts

The applicant was suffering from a fatal disease. She wanted her husband to assist her to commit suicide when this became necessary to avoid the distressing and undignified final stages of the disease. She claimed that the prohibition in domestic law on assisting suicide infringed her rights under Arts 2, 3, 8, 9 and 14 of the ECHR.

Legal principle

The ECtHR found that there had been no violation of any of the Convention rights. On the discrimination point, the court found that there had been no violation of Art. 14 because there was an 'objective and reasonable' justification for the domestic law in question, which 'was designed to safeguard life by protecting the weak and vulnerable'.

KEY CASE

ADT v UK (2001) 31 EHRR 33

Concerning: Arts. 8 and 14

Facts

The applicant claimed that his conviction for 'gross indecency' violated Arts 8 and 14. The offence in question prohibited certain homosexual sexual activity.

▶

Legal principle

The ECtHR rights held that there had been a violation of Art. 8, and that it was unnecessary to consider Art. 14. The legislation in question and applicant's conviction under it interfered with his right to respect for his private life, and that there had no justification for the prosecution in question, given the absence of any public health considerations and 'the purely private nature of the behaviour [in question]'.

Case	Decision
Dudgeon v *UK* (1981)	Prohibition of private homosexual conduct between men aged over 21 was a breach of Art. 8.
Belgian Linguistics Case (1967)	The right to education guaranteed in Art. 2 of the Protocol does not require the state to provide education in the language preferred by parents.
East African Asians v *UK* (1981)	The application of immigration procedures that discriminated on the grounds of race could, in certain circumstances, constitute degrading treatment contrary to Art. 3.
Botta v *Italy* (1998)	Article 14 is not relevant unless the facts of the case fall within the scope of one or more of the 'rights and freedoms' safeguarded by the ECHR; it has no independent existence.

 Make your answer stand out

An important issue here is whether courts are too reluctant to interfere with the decisions of democratically elected authorities. In *R (on the application of Begum)* v *Denbigh High School Governors* (2006), a case concerning the application of Art. 9 in the context of school uniforms, Lord Hoffmann stated that 'a domestic court should accept the decision of Parliament to allow individual schools to make their own decisions about uniforms'. It is arguable that this approach is too deferential to the authorities in question. See the essay by Gibson (2007).

A second important matter which you could raise concerns Protocol 12 which would fill a 'gap' in the protection against discrimination currently provided by domestic legislation and the ECHR; certain commentators argue that it should be ratified. See the articles by Fredman (2002) and Wintemute (2004).

■ Putting it all together

Answer guidelines

See the essay question at the start of the chapter.

Approaching the question

You need to start by defining the elements of the question: what exactly is discrimination? What are the main pieces of domestic legislation? In what ways does the ECHR deal with discrimination? You should explain that you will consider the adequacy of the law, and proposals for reform, in the light of academic and other debate.

Important points to include

The exact content of your answer will depend on your syllabus. You should outline the way that the Equality Act 2010 deals with discrimination, how key cases which are still relevant have interpreted the key legal requirements and the role of the Equality and Human Rights Commission in this context. You should consider the way that the domestic courts and the ECtHR have applied the ECHR in this context. Finally, you should consider the arguments for and against the current domestic and ECHR law dealing with discrimination, and consider whether it is satisfactory in the light of law reform proposals.

✓ Make your answer stand out

Virtually all of your colleagues will mention Protocol 12 to the ECHR in answering this question, and you should definitely discuss it. However, there are various ways to particularly impress examiners. First, as we have mentioned in other chapters, it is always crucial to provide clear, accurate and succinct outlines of the relevant provisions and to explain how you reached your conclusions. Secondly, consider less obvious English laws that could be used to deal with discriminatory behaviour; it is important to make it clear that other areas of law, such as criminal law in general, can be used to combat certain discriminatory behaviour. Finally, consider practical problems relating to discrimination law. Are the laws simply too complex for potential claimants to understand? Should the Equality and Human Rights Commission have an obligation to provide assistance to individual claimants? To what extent can law actually deal effectively with discrimination as a social practice?

READ TO IMPRESS

Ashtiany, S. (2011)'The Equality Act 2010: main concepts', *International Journal of Discrimination and the Law*, 11(1/2), 29–42.

Connolly, M. (2012) 'The coalition government and age discrimination', 2 *Journal of Business Law* 144–60.

Doherty, M. (2011), 'Evolutionary rather than revolutionary: the Equality Act 2010', *Business Law Review* 32(3), 52–3.

Fredman article available online: www.justice.org.uk/images/pdfs/protocol12.pdf

Gibson, N. (2007) 'Faith in the courts: religious dress and human rights', *Cambridge Law Journal*, 66(3), 657–97.

McNorrie, K. (2008) 'Human rights, conscience and public service', JLSS, 53(4), 25–6.

Middlemiss, S. (2006/7) 'Beauty's only skin deep', CIL, 8(1), 18–46.

Wintemute, R. (2004) 'Filling the Article 14 "gap": government ratification and judicial control of Protocol No. 12 ECHR: Part 2', *European Human Rights Law Review*, 5, 484–99.

www.pearsoned.co.uk/lawexpress

 Go online to access more revision support including quizzes to test your knowledge, sample questions with answer guidelines, podcasts you can download, and more!

And finally, before the exam . . .

Look back at the advice we gave you at the beginning of the book. Have you done everything we suggested?

Test Yourself

- ☐ Look at the revision checklists at the start of each chapter. Are you happy that you can now tick them all? If not, go back to the particular chapter and work through the mxaterial again. If you are still struggling, seek help from your tutor.

- ☐ Attempt the sample questions in each chapter and check your answers against the guidelines provided.

- ☐ Go online to **www.pearsoned.co.uk/lawexpress** for more hands-on revision help and try out these resources:

  - ☐ Try the **test your knowledge** quizzes and see if you can score full marks for each chapter.

  - ☐ Attempt to answer the **sample questions** for each chapter within the time limit and check your answers against the guidelines provided.

  - ☐ Listen to the **podcast** and then attempt the question it discusses.

  - ☐ **'You be the marker'** and see if you can spot the strengths and weaknesses of the sample answers.

  - ☐ Use the **flashcards** to test your recall of the legal principles of the key cases and statutes you've revised and the definitions of important terms.

  - ☐ Make sure that you have revised all the topics on your syllabus, since there is so much variance between modules at different universities. Whatever you do, do not skimp on the revision of the HRA and ECHR – these are central to any course.

■ Linking it all up

Check where there are overlaps between subject areas. (You may want to review the 'Revision note' boxes throughout this book.) Make a careful note of these, as knowing of how one topic may lead into another can increase your marks significantly. This subject is by nature one which is full of overlaps – many human rights share key concepts, and some rights must always be balanced against each other. Here are some examples:

- Chapters 1 and 2 overlap with every other chapter, since the HRA and ECHR have an impact upon each and every field of human rights.

- Freedom of expression is a feature of many chapters to differing extents.

- The exceptions to Art. 8 privacy-related rights and Art. 10 freedom of expression include each other.

- Breach of confidence is discussed in different forms in two chapters.

■ Knowing your cases

Make sure you know how to use relevant case law in your answers. Use the table below to focus your revision of the key cases in each topic. To review the details of these cases, refer back to the particular chapter.

Key case	How to use	Related topics
Chapter 1 Human Rights Act 1998		
Re McKerr (2004)	To distinguish between ECHR and HRA 1998; on non-retroactivity of HRA 1998	Article 2 ECHR right to life
R v *A* (2002)	To discuss court's role under s 3 HRA 1998	s 4 HRA 1998
Bellinger v *Bellinger* (2003)	To discuss court's role under s 3 HRA	s 4 HRA
(*Johnson*) R v *Havering LBC* (2007)	To clarify meaning of public authority under s 6 HRA	

Key case	How to use	Related topics
Chapter 2 European Convention on Human Rights		
Handyside v *UK* (1979)	To show breadth of 'margin of appreciation'	Associated with principles of interpretation of various Articles
Osman v *UK* (2000)	To explain Article 2: positive duty on state to protect life	Linked to matters involving a real and immediate risk to life
Ireland v *UK* (1978)	To explain Article 3: torture and other forms of ill-treatment	Distinguishing the difference of intensity in the suffering of the detainees.
Steel and Morris v *UK* (2005)	To explain Article 6: lack of legal aid for libel case – fair hearing?	Requirements for legal advice and representation
Saunders v *UK* (1996)	To explain Article 6: right against self-incrimination	Involuntary statements leading to an unfair trial
S*ahin* v *Turkey* (2005)	To explain Article 9: identifying problem related to manifesting one's own religion	Associated with justified interference and proportionality
Lingens v *Austria* (1986)	To explain Article 10: freedom of expression and political issues of public interest	*Jersild* v *Denmark* (1995) – publication of information in the media
Ollinger v *Austria* (2006)	To explain Article 11: opposing sides demonstrating	Public protest and freedom of expression under Article 10
Chapter 3 Police powers		
Richardson v *Chief Constable of West Midlands* (2011)	To decide whether the arrest was necessary	Requirements for arrest and detention
R v *Commissioner of Police of the Metropolis* (2011)	To discuss destruction of DNA and fingerprint samples under s 64 PACE	See *S and Marper* v *UK* (2008) – indefinite retention violation of Article 8 ▶

Key case	How to use	Related topics
R v Paris, Abdullahi, Miller (1993)	To decide whether confession made under s 76 PACE was oppression	Application of s 76 and refusal to admit evidence under s 78 PACE
R v Howard Chung (1991)	To decide whether breach of s 76 makes a confession unreliable	Section 78 and evidence having an adverse effect on the fairness of the proceedings
R v Argent (1997)	To discuss s 34 CJPOA 1994 and the right to silence	Condron v UK (2001) – being given legal advice by solicitor to remain silent

Chapter 4 Public order

Key case	How to use	Related topics
R (on the application of Laporte) v Chief Constable of Gloucestershire Constabulary (2006)	To discuss breach of the peace and the right to demonstrate	Piddington v Bates (1961) – breach of the peace and protests getting out of control under Articles 10 and 11.
Austin and Another v Commissioner of Police of the Metropolis (2009)	To discuss police preventing demonstrators from leaving area ('kettling') in order to avoid violence	Possible breach of Article 5 by deprivation of liberty
R v Mahroof (1989)	To discuss s 2 POA: for violent disorder, there must be at least three persons present involved in the criminal activity	Connected to other offences such as riot, affray and fear or provocation of violence
Dehal v CPS (2005)	To discuss s 4A POA: the offence of intentional harassment, alarm or distress	Norwood v DPP (2003): interrelated with ss 4 and 5 POA
Hammond (John) v DPP (2004)	To decide under s 5 POA decide whether a sign could be considered insulting, if not threatening, or abusive	Linked to proportionality under Article 10

Key case	How to use	Related topics
DPP v *Bayer and Others* (2004)	To apply s 68 CJPOA: reasonableness of aggravated trespass	Necessary force used against others carrying out an unlawful act
Hirst and Agu v *Chief Constable of West Yorkshire* (1987)	To apply s 137 Highways Act 1980: protestors wilfully obstructing the highway	Sections 132–138 Serious Organised Crime and Police Act 2005 – demonstrations in the vicinity of Parliament
R (Haw) v *Secretary of State for the Home Department and Another* (2006)	To apply s 134 SOCPA – authorisation for demonstration	Compatibility with 'prescribed by law' in Article 10 and 11 of the ECHR
Hall, Haw and Others v *The Mayor of London* (2010)	To decide whether order to evict demonstrators proportionate under the ECHR	Interpretation of 'necessary in a democratic society' under Articles 10 and 11 of ECHR

Chapter 5: Contempt of court

Key case	How to use	Related topics
Attorney-General v *Mirror Group Newspapers Ltd* (2012)	To interpret conditions for strict liability rule under ss 1 and 2 of the CCA 1981	Substantial risk that proceedings may be seriously impeded or prejudiced
Attorney-General v *MGN Ltd and News Group International Ltd* (1997)	To evaluate publishing stories about an arrestee, who was never charged with any offence	Publication that create a substantial risk to a fair trial
Attorney-General v *Punch* (2003)	To apply s 6 CCA : common law contempt – Intention to impede or prejudice the administration of justice	The essential elements of common law contempt of court
Attorney-General v *Scotcher* (2005)	To apply s 8 CCA – disclosing statements made in the jury room	Upholding the sanctity of the jury room
R v *Young* (1995)	To apply s 8 CCA – jury discussing case outside the jury room	Material irregularity of a jury's verdict

▶

Key case	How to use	Related topics
Interbrew SA v *Financial Times and Others* (2002)	To understand s 10 CCA – refusal to disclose source of information to the court	*Financial Times* v *UK* (2009) – protection of journalist's sources under Article 10 of the ECHR
R v *Davis* (2008)	To understand common law circumstances where witnesses may give evidence anonymously	Section 88 Coroners and Justice Act 2009 – conditions for witness anonymity

Chapter 6 Privacy

Key case	How to use	Related topics
Wainwright v *UK* (2007)	To evaluate privacy protection under English law; scope of Art. 8	Scope of Arts 3 and 13
Peck v *UK* (2003)	To evaluate privacy protection under English law; doing private things in public place	Scope of Arts 8 and 13
Lion Laboratories v *Evans* (1985)	To understand public interest defence to breach of confidence claims	
Campbell v *Mirror Group* (2004)	To apply test for privacy claims; reasonable expectation of privacy; intrusive nature of photographs	Balancing of Arts 8 and 10
Von Hannover v *Germany* (2005)	To evaluate scope of privacy protection under Art. 8; private activities carried out in public	Balancing of Arts 8 and 10
Murray v *Big Pictures* (2008)	To understand reasonable expectation of privacy; private activities carried out in public	
R v *Shayler* (2002)	To evaluate human rights implications of the Official Secrets Act 1989; availability of defences	Art. 10 ECHR and national security
R v *Keogh* (2007)	To understand Official Secrets Act 1989 – reverse burden of proof	Section 3 HRA – reading down a statute to make it ECHR-compliant

Key case	How to use	Related topics
Chapter 7 Obscenity		
R v *Anderson* (1972)	To understand meaning of 'obscene'	
DPP v *Whyte* (1972)	To understand meaning of obscene and the relevance of the audience	
R v *Calder & Boyars* (1969)	To understand public good defence under the Obscene Publications Acts	
R v *Perrin* (2002)	To understand human rights and the OPA	Scope of Arts 7 and 10
Hoare v *UK* (1997)	To understand human rights and the OPA	Scope of Art. 10
Handyside v *UK* (1979)	To understand human rights and the OPA	Basic principles of freedom of expression under Art. 10
Chapter 8 Terrorism		
Attorney-General's Reference (No. 4 of 2002) (2003)	To apply s 11 TA 2000 – burden of proof for being a member of a proscribed organisation	Section 3(4): Secretary of State may ban organisation believing it to connected to terrorism
R v *Zafar and Others* (2008)	To apply s 57 TA: intention to use articles found in possession of suspects to incite terrorism	Section 58: suspect collects or possesses documents likely to be useful for terrorism
A v *Secretary of State for the Home Department* (2004)	To discuss terrorism issues involving Articles 5, 14 and 15 of the ECHR	Detention without trial under s 23 Anti-terrorism, Crime and Security Act 2001
A and Others v *UK* (2009)	To discuss terrorism issues involving Articles 3, 5, 14 and 15 of the ECHR	Control orders under s 1 of the Prevention of Terrorism Act 2005

▶

Key case	How to use	Related topics
Secretary of State for the Home Department v *JJ and Others* (2007)	To discuss whether control orders imposed deprived individuals of their right to liberty	Non-derogating control orders and the right to liberty in Article 5 ECHR
A and Others v *UK* (2009)	To discuss whether applicants were prevented from properly assessing the lawfulness of their detention under Article 5(4) and closed material	Related to Terrorist Prevention and Investigation Measures Act 2011
Secretary of State for the Home Department v *MB and AF* (2007)	To discuss issues involved whether defendants received a fair trial under Article 6 of the ECHR	Whether control orders sufficiently protected against breach of Article 6 in relation to 'closed material'
R v *Da Costa; R* v *Ahmet; R* v *Hamid; R* v *Ahmed; R* v *Al-Figari* (2009)	To understand ss 5, 6 and 8 of the Terrorism Act 2006	

Chapter 9 Discrimination

Mandla v *Dowell Lee* (1983)	To understand indirect racial discrimination	
London Borough of Lewisham v *Malcolm* (2008)	To critique the old law of disability discrimination	Changes under Equality Act 2010
Eweida v *BA* (2010)	To understand indirect discrimination; religious discrimination	Appropriate comparators in discrimination law
Burden v *UK* (2007)	To discuss discrimination under Art. 14 ECHR in combination with Art. 1 of First Protocol	
Abdulaziz, Cabales and Balkandani v *UK* (1985)	To discuss discrimination under Art. 14 ECHR	Scope of Arts 3 and 8

Key case	How to use	Related topics
Pretty v *UK* (2002)	To discuss discrimination under Art. 14 ECHR	Arts 2, 3, 8 and 9
ADT v *UK* (2001)	To discuss discrimination under Art. 14 ECHR	Art. 8 ECHR

▌Sample question

Below is a sample problem question that incorporates overlapping areas of the law. See if you can answer this question, drawing upon your knowledge of the whole subject area. Guidelines on answering this question are included at the end of this section.

PROBLEM QUESTION

On Thursday evening the organisers of the anti-smoking group Freedom Against Smoking (FAGS) learn that free cigarettes are being given away at a nearby tobacconist shop, in order to promote a new brand. Four members of FAGS, John, Paula (who is the chairperson), Georgina and Richard decide to demonstrate peaceably outside the shop.

The next morning John displays pictures of cancerous stomachs and lungs to passersby outside the shop and shouts, 'This could happen to you if you smoke'. Two young children who are walking by are visibly sick at the sight of the pictures. The police arrive and ask the protestors to disperse. They refuse. PC Brown recognises John, whom he had arrested six months earlier for traffic violations, puts his hand on John's shoulder and says, 'You know the drill, let's go'.

Another police constable, PC White, notices that Georgina has put something into her pocket. He immediately approaches her and says, 'I am going to search you. I believe that you have in your possession something that could be used in connection with terrorism'. After he finds a book about Islam entitled *No More Wars* and a letter postmarked Afghanistan in her bag, she is immediately arrested, without being given any specific reasons.

PC Green receives a message from his duty officer at the police station to immediately arrest Richard for robbery. As he attempts to do so Richard verbally protests. PC Smith

▶

throws him onto the ground and then handcuffs him. At the police station Richard is placed in a cell and kept there for 15 hours without being interviewed. His request for a solicitor is initially denied on the grounds that the investigating officers are busy with a murder inquiry. When Richard is eventually questioned, the police continually shout at him telling him that he had better admit to the robbery or else he will go prison for so long that he will not see his children again for at least 12 years. Richard then confesses.

During the demonstration Paula confides in Richard that she has been smoking secretly 40 cigarettes a day for some 20 years. However, she is now attending a private health treatment centre and for the past week has been having hypnotherapy sessions to help her give up the habit. Richard is so disappointed that he informs the *Daily Rag Mag*. The following day the headline in the newspaper reads 'Paula Puffs Forty a Day'. The article discusses her treatment and emphasises the dangers of smoking. On the following page there is a news item about a trial that has commenced concerning a cigarette manufacturer who is being sued by someone who contracted cancer. The Attorney-General issues proceedings against the newspaper for contempt of court.

(1) John is eventually convicted under ss 4, 4A and 5 of the POA 1986.

(2) Georgina is convicted under s 58 of the Terrorism Act 2000.

(3) Richard pleads guilty to robbery.

(4) Paula decides to sue Richard for breach of confidence.

(5) The *Daily Rag Mag* is found guilty of contempt of court.

Advise all the parties involved.

Answer guidelines

Approaching the question

This question is designed as an aid to revision of as many human rights issues as possible. Don't panic – it is not likely that you will ever see such a broad question on an exam paper! If you can answer this question, you should feel confident about your own exam.

Important points to include

We have tried to incorporate as many human rights issues as we possibly could. Hence, you should have spotted police powers; public order offences; terrorism; privacy (breach of confidence); contempt of court. However, hopefully you will also have recognised that there are literally dozens of other issues involved and which are to be discussed throughout the question, including various ECHR Articles (especially Arts 3, 5, 6, 8, 10), as well as the various domestic statutes and common law problems arising in each issue.

 Make your answer stand out

Even though this is a problem question, it does contain opportunities to demonstrate that you have read widely. Which of the points in the question are uncertain? Which have current reform proposals? You should be able to spot that we suggested further reading on some of the issues raised in the question, and told you how to use it! For example, there are some very recent materials on contempt of court in this book, which could be helpful in your answer.

Glossary of terms

The key definitions can be found within the chapter in which they occur as well as in the glossary below. These definitions are the essential terms that you must know and understand in order to prepare for an exam.

Damaging disclosure under OSA 1989, ss 1–4	'Damaging' means that the disclosure has damaged, or is likely to damage, one of the listed state interests in the relevant section.
Different types of offences	Offences are divided into three categories depending, in general terms, on their seriousness.
Direct discrimination	'Direct' discrimination consists of less favourable treatment on prohibited grounds. Thus, a person commits direct sex discrimination against a woman if 'on the ground of her sex he treats her less favourably than he treats or would treat a man'.
For gain	It is clear that the gain in question does not have to be for the defendant; 'gain for another' is sufficient (Obscene Publications Act 1959, s 2(1), as amended by the 1964 Act). However, the legislation does not define 'gain'. Financial benefit will count, but other sorts of gain, such as the receipt of pleasure derived from the article, may also suffice.
Indirect discrimination	'Indirect' discrimination concerns requirements, conditions, provisions, criteria, or practices that are apparently neutral but which have a significantly disproportionate and unjustifiable adverse effect on members of a particular group.

Obscene

An article is obscene 'if its effect or (where the article comprises two or more distinct items) the effect of any of its items is, if taken as a whole, such as to tend to deprave and corrupt persons who are likely, having regard to all relevant circumstances, to read, see or hear the matter contained or embodied in it'.

Positive discrimination

'Positive discrimination' is treatment which favours a particular group in order to try to eliminate an existing inequality between this group and another.

Proportionality

Proportionality is a tool that the court uses to balance the competing interests in the particular situation before them. In essence, the court considers whether the exercise of the power of the state could have been carried out in a way which interferes less with the exercise of the rights of the individual. If the same result could have been achieved with less interference, the measures the state took will be disproportionate and therefore will breach the Convention.

Public authority

A body whose functions are public (expressly including courts and tribunals), or whose functions are partly public in nature. Where a body's functions are only partly public in nature, then it is only bound by s 6 HRA 1998 in respect of its public functions.

Public good

Section 4(1) of the OPA 1959 creates a 'public good' defence: it stipulates that a defendant shall not be liable 'if it is proved that publication of the article in question is justified as being for the public good on the ground that it is in the interests of science, literature, art or learning, or of other objects of general concern'.

Reasonable expectation of privacy

The requirement since *Campbell* (2004) for bringing a claim in breach of confidence/misuse of private information. It depends on all the circumstances of the individual case.

Reasonable grounds for suspicion

Reasonable suspicion is an objective test; reasonableness is not assessed simply by reference to the constable's opinion.

Victimisation

'Victimisation' for complaining about discrimination in good faith is itself a form of discrimination. The legislation on discrimination contains specific provisions designed to protect people from this kind of victimisation. These provisions protect those who complain about discrimination in good faith, as well as various other people: for example, those who provide evidence or information in good faith in connection with proceedings brought against an alleged discriminator.

Terrorism under TA 2000, s 1

In general terms, terrorism means the use or threat of action which:

■ causes some damage – against a person or property – or threatens to cause that damage;

■ AND which is designed to influence the government or the general public;

■ AND which is made to advance a political, religious or ideological cause.

Under s 40, a terrorist is anyone who commits an offence under the 2000 Act, or who is or has been involved in the commission, preparation or instigation of acts of terrorism.

Index